THE JOB SYNDROME

DIVINING THE MYSTERY OF MISERY

JOHN R. MILLER

ALL PEOPLES MINISTRIES
LYNCHBURG, VA

The Job Syndrome: Divining The Mystery of Misery

Published by All Peoples Ministries
P.O. Box 3034
Lynchburg, Virginia 24503
www.allpeoplesministries.org

Copyright © 2020 John R. Miller

All rights reserved. This book is protected by the copyright laws of the United States of America. This book may not be copied or reprinted for commercial gain or profit.

Cover photo, Jerusalem at night, taken by John R. Miller
Cover design by Samuel C. Petty
Headshot taken by Robert Williams

ISBN: 978-0-9987608-6-5

Printed in the United States of America

DEDICATION

It would be only a partial truth to say that the DNA of Ralph and Hazel Miller made me who I am. They added to the DNA love, teaching, discipline, and leadership by example as to what meaningful Christian living should be. My dad, Ralph, contributed the desire to study and learn, while my mother, Hazel, showed me that prayer really does change things. So, with great love and respect, I dedicate these pages to my parents who were in large part the inspiration and source of the thoughts written here. They are missed so very much.

TRANSLATIONS

KJV Unless otherwise noted, all Scripture quotations are taken from the *Holy Bible*, King James Version.

NKJV Scripture quotations marked (NKJV) are taken from the *Holy Bible*, New King James Version®. Copyright © 1982 by Thomas Nelson, Inc. Used by permission. All rights reserved.

NIV Scripture quotations marked (NIV) are taken from the *Holy Bible*, New International Version®, NIV®. Copyright © 1973, 1978, 1984, 2011 by Biblica, Inc.™ Used by permission of Zondervan. All rights reserved worldwide. www.zondervan.com The "NIV" and "New International Version" are trademarks registered in the United States Patent and Trademark Office by Biblica, Inc.™

NASB Scripture quotations marked (NASB) are taken from the New American Standard Bible®, Copyright © 1960, 1962, 1963, 1968, 1971, 1972, 1973, 1975, 1977, 1995 by The Lockman Foundation. Used by permission. www.Lockman.org

Tanakh Scripture quotations marked (Tanakh) are taken from *Tanakh: The Holy Scriptures* (Jerusalem: The Jewish Publication Society, 1985). The *Tanakh* is the Jewish Bible published by the Jewish Publication Society.

Gordis Translated by Robert Gordis in either *The Book of God and Man* (Chicago: University of Chicago Press, 1830) or *The Book of Job: Commentary, New Translation, Special Studies* (New York: The Jewish Theological Seminary Press, 2012).

Clines Translated by David J. A. Clines in *Job 1-20*, Word Biblical Commentary, vol. 17 (Nashville, TN: Nelson Reference Electronic, 1989).

Dhorme Translated by Édouard Dhorme in *Commentary on the Book of Job* (Nashville: Thomas Nelson, 1984).

Hartley Translated by John E. Hartley in *The Book of Job,* New International Commentary on the Old Testament (Grand Rapids: Eerdmans, 1988).

Pope Translated by Marvin Pope in *Job,* The Anchor Bible, vol. 15 (New York: Doubleday & Company, 1965).

CONTENTS

	Preface	1
1	**The Problem with the Book of Job** *A Questioning of What is Fair*	6
	-The Job Syndrome	8
	-Seeing the Need	11
	-The Problem: Innocent Suffering and the Doctrine of Retribution	13
	-My Prayer	22
2	**An Overview of the Book of Job** *A Limp in Your Life Not by Your Choice*	23
	-Structure, Location and Characters of Job	33
	-Literary Considerations	49
	-The Purpose of the Book of Job	53
	-My Prayer	55
3	**Evidences of the Job Syndrome**	56
	-Background and World-view of Job	63
	-Job's Syndrome	69
	-My Prayer	75
4	**The Theology of the Book of Job: Part One**	76
	-Introductory Thoughts to the Theology of Job	88
	-The Validity of the Book of Job	91
	-The Worship of One God in Job	93
	-The Attributes of God in the Book of Job	96
	-Evil or Suffering in Job	106
	-My Prayer	112

5	**The Theology of the Book of Job: Part Two**	**114**
	-The Theology of Job	129
	-Rahab	130
	-Behemoth	132
	-Leviathan	136
	-My Prayer	145
6	**Conclusions Toward Solutions**	**146**
	-Job's Example	159
	-Dealing with Self in the Process	162
	-My Prayer	165
7	**Divining the Truth About the God of Job**	**166**
	-Perceiving the God of Job	177
	-Modern Ministry to the Job Syndrome	184
	-A Happy Ending	189
	-My Prayer	193
8	**Father Does Know Best**	**194**
	-The Art of Waiting	195
	-Organized Attacks	200
	-Insight from Outside Christian Writing	202
	-Deep Things Out of Darkness (Job 12:22)	204
	-A Final Word	205
	-My Prayer	207
	Notes	209
	Selected Bibliography	215
	Acknowledgements	221

PREFACE

Recently, I was awakened from a disturbing dream. No, it wasn't from lobster or hotdogs. It was just a simple dream that had me fleeing from a supposed danger. I was walking through a car repair garage trying to find an individual. From one area, two men started toward me. I then noticed two other men from a different area who also began to approach. I could tell their intent was not good. My only hope was to run to the corner of the nearby streets, get into a high traffic area and try to draw attention from anyone in order to get help. The problem with that was the fact that being many years senior to these young and agile men I did not think I could escape them. I awoke in the process of fleeing. One of the most basic reactions to threat is flight. All of us have "been there and done that." That dream holds no great revelatory truth to me, but it is important to the very essence of this book.

Believers in all the many facets of the Christian faith have experiences in life, which threaten their well-being and peace. No true Christian escapes! Life is not fair, not even for the most committed and faithful among us. We have learned, "He causes His sun to rise on the evil and the good, and sends rain on the righteous and the unrighteous." (Matthew 5:45, NASB) In fact, quite often it is the saint most actively seeking God who experiences the most awful pain in reversals and calamity.

Here enters the paradigm of saints who suffer, Job. This grand old man of the Old Testament was a real patriarch who, in spite of massive losses and physical pain, remained faithful to God and never gave up. In his case, there was no time for flight. He was attacked from all sides in every matter that was truly important to him. Even Job's wife tried to persuade him to take the quick way out—death.

This book is an examination of the heart, mind, and attitude of the man God chose to exemplify patience in suffering. More importantly, the Book of Job reveals truths about Job's God and His relationship to Job, which are critical to understanding the dynamics of a soul in suffering. Suffering happens! But, in the whirlwind of life, God will reveal Himself to those who have suffered to the breaking point and beyond.

I have always had a fascination with the Book of Job. It began in my childhood during a period when I had multiple boils in my body, a disease with a striking similarity to Job's malady. So, when I needed to write a dissertation for the Doctor of Ministry degree, I asked for the privilege of using this wonderful book as my subject. I knew of no other source of material that dealt with one of the areas where ministry is most needed—suffering. The thoughts, observations, and even theological concepts found here were not born in a few days at the beginning of a life of ministry. They were chiseled, hammered, and formed throughout my many years of "rubber meeting the road" ministry, dealing with real people, even saints, having real problems.

I have taken many of the basic tenets of the dissertation, "The Job Syndrome," and laid them out here in more readable and devotional style. This book is not a verse-by-verse commentary of Job. There are so many of those already. Neither is it a systematic theology, even though certain theological concepts do strengthen the contents. This is not an attempt to explain why Job had his problems. I do not believe the Book of Job explains why. I do not see a "one size fits all" answer to the question, "Why?" There are so many emotions, struggles, insights, doubts, questions, and revelations, which come to a suffering believer. The man Job and his story, his philosophy, and his devotion are on the one hand extraordinary and on the other hand typical. Job's processes are our processes. I call him the archetype of a believing sufferer, the preeminent example.

Christian believers who are suffering calamity, or those who have ever suffered life threatening or soul jarring catastrophe, will be the primary beneficiaries of this book. Those who minister to sufferers will also find the pages here to contain concepts, encouragements, and models, which may be used to empathetically touch the lives of those in stress and distress. After all, it is vital for ministers to be true "comforters" and not join the ranks of Job's so-called "comforters" who actually became antagonists accusing Job of wrongdoing.

Although each chapter can be read autonomously, there is some sequence to the ideas of the book as they build on each other, "precept upon precept" (Isaiah 28:10). An example is the doctrine of retribution, which is the reward, either good or bad, expected for obedience or disobedience. One of Job's major frustrations is the seeming contradiction to this belief in just reward. Another illustration is Job's belief system. His faith, in the form of trust, is tried to its limit, but there is a process of shaking and sifting, or better, a purifying until his trust in God is stronger than ever at the end of his experience.

A disclaimer is appropriate here. All of the stories included in this book are true accounts of real events that happened to real people. (A few fictitious names and places have been used in order to maintain the anonymity of those involved, but all but one of the main characters feature real names.) These are the real stories of people in my life who have experienced their own Job syndromes.

In the writing of this book over the past eight years, I have undergone all the symptoms of a Job syndrome. One must determine whether to keep marching or not. I am so glad I kept marching. Now there is an almost overwhelming sense of resolution in knowing I too have been to the whirlwind and met God.

My cousin, Jim, described the journey so beautifully in

an unpublished poem, which he graciously allowed me to use here. As we embark, listen!

Island in the Soul

In agony of my life
I call out and can find no answer.
No philosopher, no engineer, no magician
Aids me and there is no recourse.
Solace eludes me and despair binds me
Amidst seas unknown
Alone, on a lost Island in My Soul.
But on the sharp, cutting stones of this desert shore
I find a footprint and then another
I look up and there stands Job, smiling,
"Come," he says, "I can show you the way."

Jim Armstrong, 5/19/2014

1
THE PROBLEM WITH THE BOOK OF JOB
A QUESTIONING OF WHAT IS FAIR

> I have rejected my life;
>   so I can give vent to my complaint,
>   speak out of the bitterness of my soul.
> I will say to God, Do not hold me guilty;
>   but tell me why you are my adversary.
> Do you take pleasure in oppression,
>   in rejecting the work of your own hands,
>   while smiling on the plans of the wicked?
>   -Job 10:1-3 (Clines)[1]

The year was 1969. I was in my first full-time pastorate. One of the charter members, Mrs. Dubose, became sick and was bedfast. Only a few months before, I had preached the funeral of her saintly husband. Now this precious and faithful believer was suffering from what we later learned to be congestive heart failure. In a private conversation, she asked, "Pastor, what should I do?" Her countenance and tone were desperate. There was a disturbed agony in her question and tears in her eyes. She went on to explain that her family, which was only a nephew and niece-in-law, wanted her to call for a doctor. What was her problem with that? She had never been to a doctor or taken any kind of medication, not even an aspirin, since her salvation experience in 1923, but she had trusted God for healing and health. She had lived by faith, and obviously, it had worked for her up to this point in her life. What does a young pastor say? I was so stunned that I really have no memory of my response. I must have encouraged her to follow the wishes of her nephew, since that is what occurred. Within weeks, I preached the funeral of this precious saint.

That event began a journey in discovering the meaning of 1 Peter 1:7, "That the trial of your faith, being more precious than of gold that perisheth, though it be tried with fire, might be found unto the praise and honor and glory at the appearing of Jesus Christ." On her deathbed, Mrs. Dubose was tried in her faith. Tried in what she actually believed to be true about God and His promises. This same kind of trial of faith has been my personal experience on several occasions, and I have observed it in the lives of saints again and again. I am not talking about the numerous irritations and hiccups in our Christian walk, but the life-shaking and faith-challenging kind of trial that brings one to the brink of total apostasy.

Job, the man, is the preeminent example of a faithful sufferer. Only the passion of Jesus our Christ supersedes the paradigm of Job in teaching the modern Christian believer the reality of suffering and a proper response to it. When the impoverished, afflicted, and contradicted Job uttered the despairing statements quoted above, his focus had turned from the loss of wealth and family, along with his excruciating bodily disease, to his feeling of abandonment by God. In fact, Job was sensing that this same God, who formerly dealt with him in favor, provision, health, and prosperity, had now become his enemy with a determination to do nothing to change his plight. He asked if God was taking some kind of pleasure in oppressing him and rejecting him even though he was created by God's own hands. Job was so confused, frustrated, and pained that he was motivated to risk his life to vent his complaint and express the bitterness, which, like the boils in his body, was trying to fester in his soul.

The Job Syndrome

The American Heritage Dictionary of the English Language has as its secondary meaning of the word "syndrome" this definition, "A complex of symptoms indicating the existence of an undesirable condition or quality."[2] It is to this "complex of symptoms" in Job's very undesirable experience that our attention will be drawn. As in Job's life, when our lives are turned upside down by tragic circumstances, the meaning of life comes into very clear focus. Often, we re-evaluate and even question our relationship with God, especially why His promises are not immediately fulfilled in coming to our rescue.

Job's theological position was the same as that of his friends relative to the scriptural principle known as the law or doctrine of retribution. They believed and lived by the concept that righteous and good work is rewarded, and that evil and sinful living is punished. It was Job's unexpected experience of loss and extreme suffering that caused him to re-think his theology. Still, he never ceased to believe in the sovereignty of God, nor did he doubt at all his own innocence. Job's trial had a three-pronged gig effect deeply wounding him. The loss of all his animal holdings, along with his servants with whom he had strong ties, was an enormous blow emotionally. Then, the losses of his children brought an even deeper debilitating sorrow. Finally, his own excruciatingly painful disease tore away at any vestiges of emotional stamina, as the pain demanded his attention every minute of his existence. These barbs of evil were stuck fast in Job, the most righteous man in the world at that time.

The reality in the book of Job is that the main character is both unique and common. Job is unique in that no other Bible character or person of history has suffered in the same way as Job, and he was obviously chosen by God as a paradigm. In contrast, Job's commonality with all believers is to be seen and understood in the principles responsible for the fact of and the proper response to suffering. Job is neither the first man Adam (1 Cor. 15:45) in whom all mankind is fallen; nor, is he the second man Jesus Christ (1 Cor. 15:47) who provided redemption for all creation including those fallen people who call on Him. Yet, **Job is uniquely everyman. He is the archetype of all believers who suffer.** In Job's example, we shall see that, according to the Scripture, all who set their course to live for God will go through experiences of suffering.

> In fact, everyone who wants to live a godly life in Christ Jesus will be persecuted.
> -2 Timothy 3:12 (NIV)

If Job, the man, is the paradigm of faithfulness in endurance of suffering (the historical interpretation of the Church), then Job, the book, should offer instruction and guidance to solutions for the questions it exposes about suffering, especially innocent suffering, and evil. It should also reveal God's place and function in relation to those who suffer. One of the surprising facts is that nowhere in the book does it explicitly answer either of those questions about innocent suffering and evil. As will be seen later in this writing, **the life-applicable principles of living faithfully before God are hidden in the existential experience of Job's life.** The mysteries must be sought out with very careful exegesis of the text or, more plainly, a rock-solid interpretation of what is actually written in the book. **The author of Job made no attempt to be didactic in the general sense of the term. He was not laying out a lesson or teaching great principles of theology. He was telling the story of a man, his loses, his suffering, his discourses with friends, and his final confrontation with God.** The story is real, but its great truths are to be discovered primarily in the symbolisms used in the book and in Job's encounter with God. **Many times, these truths can only be learned through a Job-**

like experience of suffering.

Even after thorough investigations by numerous commentators, both ancient and modern, as to the innocent suffering of Job, the haunting question of "why," is left unanswered except in partial and inadequate explanations. For centuries, writers have addressed the human need to know why, but in Job's case, that was never answered, even after God made His presence known in His appearance to Job. Claude E. Cox, a skilled interpreter, observed, "God keeps the answers to the big questions an impenetrable mystery."[3] **The "mystery" in unanswered questions is one of the significant characteristics of a Job syndrome.** Since the answer to the question "why" shall, in most cases, remain a mystery in the sovereign will of God, here it is my mission to share some of the discoveries I have made that will give light through the dark and lonely valley of extreme suffering. I want to identify the principles that guided Job and to propose a methodology of "working through" those principles by those who in their present circumstances are living out the Job syndrome. Here you will not find a five-, seven-, or even twelve-step method to freedom, but **you will find encouragement to trust our all-wise Father and to hold on until all hope is gone—then, hold on some more!**

Seeing the Need

Eleven years had gone by without a child coming into our home. In surprise and joy, the doctor's news confirming a pregnancy changed our circumstances dramatically. It was the Friday after the Thanksgiving holiday that an eight-pound five ounce, absolutely beautiful baby boy had to be delivered by caesarean section because his heart was in distress. Our joy quickly turned to anxious concern for our son. He did not breathe on his own for over seven minutes. His lungs were coated internally seriously hindering the absorption of oxygen due to his aspirating meconium in the birth process. Our baby boy, Gabriel, was breathing at over one hundred and fifty respirations per minute. He was seriously ill. Within twenty-four hours, Gabriel was flown to a neo-natal intensive care unit in another city. After two days of testing, the doctor's report was devastating, "If he survives, he will be hospitalized at least three months due to his breathing problems and the brain damage." On the following Tuesday morning sitting in a hospital chapel, I faced my own Job syndrome!

What does one do? What is the right path of response? **I was facing the biggest trial of my life armed only with the typical array of answers so often spoken in the Christianese of modern "ministry." In the midst of painful and desperate circumstances, even in the life of one consecrated to God, words fail!** How can a minister positively guide and encourage a person who is going through such a trial of faith? Despite Bible school or seminary training and sometimes years of good and faithful service, most ministers can relate experiences of awkwardness and inadequacy at times of extreme stress and suffering in the lives of others. Filled with well-rehearsed clichés and often-used scriptural quotations, such a minister may seem to be no more helpful than Job's friends who pontificated their pat but mistaken theologies of the justice and retribution of God. When we are in the pain of devastation, neither you nor I need to hear the sugar-coated platitudes of how fair God is.

God is not necessarily fair, but He is wholly right! He Who is holy, holy, holy, is eternally right. Fair is a word, which relates to man's temporal perspective. **Right is a word, which relates to God's eternal perspective.** Fair is based on a human judgment, while right proceeds from God's absolute righteousness. In other words, **fair may or may not be right, but right is always unequivocally and unconditionally right.** As we look more and more into the Job syndrome, the understanding of these terms will become clearer. This does contradict much of the current theology, but **I am thoroughly convinced that when we come to a revelation of Father's "rightness," we will quit demanding that He be fair.** In fact, I will press the point even further. **There is a self-centered idolatry in demanding God use our sense of fair instead of His sense of right.**

The Problem:
Innocent Suffering and the Doctrine of Retribution

God, through His servant Moses, in the book of Deuteronomy teaches, "And all these blessings shall come on thee, and overtake thee, if thou shalt hearken unto the voice of the Lord thy God" (Deut. 28:2). The passage goes on to list a number of obediences to God, which will be rewarded with blessing. That is the positive or reward side of the doctrine of retribution. The negative or punishment side of retribution is contrasted in the same chapter, "But if you do not obey the Lord your God to observe faithfully all His commandments and laws which I enjoin upon you this day, all these curses shall come upon you and take effect" (Deut. 28:15, Tanakh).

The protagonists of the dialogues in the book of Job, who were indeed Job's friends, did not at all get everything wrong. They were right that suffering is many times disciplinary, and in a broader sense retributive, but they were wrong to maintain that purpose as exclusive. Job is an innocent sufferer. He is preeminently righteous for "there is none like him in the earth" (Job 1:8; 2:3); yet he suffers ultimate losses in four areas: (1) his material wealth, (2) his family (his children literally and his wife emotionally), (3) his health, and (4) his seeming abandonment by God. Herein lies the problem seen in the dialogue occupying the majority of the book (chapters 3-37, especially 3-27), the doctrine of retribution, which is both taught and illustrated throughout scripture, is contradicted by Job's experience and his discourses.

The seeming discrepancy between scriptural teaching and our Job syndrome experiences is colossal! It is baffling to the mind, devastating to the emotions, and dangerously challenging to our faith. **I believe that within the resolution of this conflict, which is both earthly and cosmic, are the truths about innocent suffering which**

can and should be applied to those hurting ones today who are in the agony of their own Job syndrome.

From the time of Adam and Eve's disobedience in eating the forbidden fruit, the Bible illustrates the consequences of disobedience. Contrastingly, in the blessings of prosperity of Abraham, Isaac, and Jacob, the reward of faithfulness is also clearly modeled. The doctrine of retribution is basically restated by the apostle Paul, "Be not deceived, God is not mocked: for whatsoever a man soweth, that shall he also reap." (Gal. 6:7). There are many other scriptural evidences of the doctrine of retribution with which observant believers are thoroughly familiar. Without going into detail at this point, two contrasting observations will be made to illustrate the problem of retribution as it is ultimately related to Job's innocent suffering.

First, it must be understood that *Yahweh*'s covenant through Moses to Israel (in the above Deuteronomic passage as well as others) must not be seen as all-inclusive. The elements of the covenant are specific to commandments and laws. Not every evil or sinful act is delineated, nor is every good and righteous work set forth. As any lawyer would explain, if it is not in the contract, it does not apply. **If one biblical example can be proven to be contradictory to the always applicable and the all-inclusive nature of the doctrine of retribution, then a serious modification of understanding of that doctrine is demanded.** Job is that contradiction. (There are other biblical examples, which are discussed below.) The

Deuteronomic covenant must have some limitations. It cannot be as simple as all bad behavior will be punished and all good behavior will be rewarded all the time, every time, anywhere, everywhere, with anyone, and everyone. R.L. Alden in his excellent commentary explained:

> Deuteronomy, Proverbs, and isolated passages throughout the Old Testament clearly teach that you get what you deserve, you reap what you sow, and you succeed or fail on the basis of your behavior. Sin will be punished, and trust and obedience will be rewarded . . . The patriarch from Uz, however, did not fit the pattern. He was a righteous man who suffered as if he were guilty of great wickedness.[4]

Second, the law of sowing and reaping is not as exacting and inflexible as it is traditionally taught. In the natural world, any farmer or gardener can explain the unpredictability of reaping and the numerous contingencies, which affect the outcome of the expected crop. I have a friend who owns blueberry fields. Last year he had a fantastic crop, but this year, due to a smaller crop and an unstable market, his reaping was not so rewarding. After doing everything agricultural science teaches, Harry is very aware of his total dependence on God for the production of a good harvest.

Jeremiah presented a controverted idea when he wrote, "They have sown wheat, but shall reap thorns" (Jer. 12:13). Micah prophesied, "Thou shalt sow, but thou shalt not reap" (Micah 6:15), again stressing the unpredictability of the principle of sowing and reaping. Jesus, Himself, made this statement, "And herein is that saying true, one soweth, and another reapeth." And continuing He stated, "I sent you to reap that whereon ye bestowed no labor: other men labored, and ye are entered into their labors," (John 4:37-38). Clearly, these scriptures and the very nature of the metaphor of sowing and reaping show that **the expected outcomes of experiences are not always commensurate to the promises of God WITHIN OUR TIMETABLES.**

This brief introduction to the doctrine of retribution, and the problem it posed to Job as he suffered his multiple agonies, will be expanded further as we journey with Job through his syndrome. The truth is that **retribution is clearly taught in scripture and it deals with many, even most, of the interactions of men with God and God with men.** But, Job stands as an archetype of the innocent sufferer. The man who was the most righteous suffered the worst evils as if he were the most wicked, while through the entire experience he remained a faithful servant of God. It was God Himself Who said to Job's argumentative friends, "…My wrath is kindled against thee…for ye have not spoken of me the thing that is right, as my servant Job hath." (Job 42:7) **The reality Job presents is that at times God does work outside the box of retributive justice. That fact must be added to an understanding of God's ways with men.** These two concepts, which seem to contradict so much of current teaching on faith, are basic to interpreting the book of Job and grasping the import of Job's test. Francis I. Anderson, whose commentary has been a wonderful source of inspiration and insight to me, astutely explained:

> ...the moral question central to Job arises from the biblical teaching that a man reaps what he sows—in this life. Rewards for virtue and punishments for vice cannot all be postponed to heaven and hell. But troubles and benefits are not distributed to mankind by an even-handed justice, it would seem. The wicked prosper, the righteous suffer. Evil is not always—not often!—punished in proportion to guilt; good is not always—not often!—rewarded in proportion to merit. The case of Job precipitates the test of faith in its severest form—the supremely righteous man who sustains the most extreme calamities. How can he, or anyone, continue to believe that God is right and fair in what He sometimes does to people? There can be no doubt that it is God, only God, who is responsible for all that happens to Job. It cannot be blamed on "Nature" or the Devil, for these are but His creatures.[5]

It was such a test of faith, similar to Job's, that we faced, as our infant son, Gabriel, lay wired to monitors and being ventilated while he struggled for every breath at the rate of 155 breaths per minute. While my good and godly wife lay at home recovering from the caesarean surgery, I sat in the hospital chapel, seeking for a thought, a word, or a scripture that would bring some hope and encouragement, **I called out to my God Who was not**

talking to me. I felt abandoned. My emotions were shattered. As I took my Bible from my briefcase and opened it again and again, it just lay there cold, dry, and meaningless. **It was my moment of destiny—the rest of my life was hanging in a balance teetering between "yes" and "no" to God's divine purpose for me and my family.** In those hours on an otherwise normal Tuesday morning, it was not my son's test, for he was the infant. It was not my wife's test although she was struggling with her own test with physical and emotional pain while dealing with her faith as well. It was my "trial of faith!"

When I put that "dead" Bible back in the briefcase, I noticed my notes from the message I had preached for the community Thanksgiving service the Wednesday evening prior to Gabriel's birth. The service was sponsored by the Ministerial Association of the city. I had preached from the Psalms on reasons to be thankful. The text for the message was Psalm 118:1 "O give thanks unto the Lord; for he is good: because his mercy endureth for ever." I felt that I needed to preach to myself, so I picked up the notes and began to read. The more I read the more I felt that I had been so wrong for not giving God thanks for giving us a son. I had been so occupied with the stressful circumstances that I had not lived up to my own sermon. After going through a litany of the wondrous acts of God, the Psalmist wrote these words:

> I will praise thee: for thou hast heard me, and art become my salvation. The stone which the builders

refused is become the head stone of the corner. This is the Lord's doing; it is marvelous in our eyes. This is the day which the Lord hath made; we will rejoice and be glad in it.

-Psalm 118:21-24

When I read through the notes and as I contemplated those Holy Spirit inspired words of the Psalmist, the message came alive to me. I broke and wept convulsively begging God's forgiveness for my attitude and not recognizing His "goodness" in our lives.

You have to understand that I did not come to that place without carrying some baggage of my own. In the months before Gabriel's birth, I had asked God to give us a baby with a healthy mind. I had struggled since being a child as I observed parents with mentally handicapped children. I could not stand the thought of possibly having to deal with a mentally challenged child. Now, I was facing with deep emotional pain the fact of the doctor's report that Gabriel was brain damaged. As I continued to convulse in mourning my "loss" and my sin of unthankfulness, I said to my Father, "I want my son! I want you to spare his life. I want Gabriel in our lives whether brain damaged or not. Give my son life, and I will give him back to You." From that moment, I began to thank God for the lives of both my son and my wife.

I do not remember how long I continued to give Him thanks for these and so many other blessings, but when I did walk out of the chapel, my life was changed totally. I was actually elated with the challenge of purpose—to be the best father I could possibly be. Amazingly, the next morning Gabriel's breathing rate had dropped into the 130's. Every day after that it dropped significantly more. The critically ill child that was supposed to be in the hospital for ninety days or more was brought home on the thirteenth day. The brain-damaged infant has never shown signs of any brain damage. He currently holds a Ph.D. in music theory and teaches at one of the largest Christian universities in America. He has more recently given me the most wonderful grandsons, Bowden and Jude. Personally, I do not believe these blessings would be mine today if I had not passed the test in the experience of my own Job syndrome.

I have now laid out the groundwork of what the Job syndrome is all about. I eagerly anticipate our journey into the dynamics of why good people sometimes suffer the most awful tragedy and pain. We will come to see that **only an expanded and more accurate understanding of God's character and His ways will motivate confidence in Him in times of extreme trouble.** My real goal in this writing is to motivate confidence in our Father. In other words, we must get our theology right before we can faithfully endure our own Job syndrome or try to minister to others who are in the throes of desperation. Ultimately, it will only be a Job-like encounter with God that will bring sense and peace to a distressed spirit. In the deepest darkness, one should expect that moment of enlightenment when, along with Job, it may be said worshipfully to *Yahweh*, "I have heard of You by the hearing of the ear; But now my eye sees You" (Job 42:5, NASB).

MY PRAYER

Omniscient Father, deep inside I know You have my ultimate and eternal welfare clearly mapped in Your plan for me. My problem with that is I am dealing with my humanity living itself out in a material world. Like Job, I know You know "the way that I take." Please help me to maintain complete confidence in that truth even when I do not see my way. Here—now! I commit to seeing You!

2
AN OVERVIEW OF THE BOOK OF JOB
A LIMP IN YOUR LIFE NOT BY YOUR CHOICE

> Oh, that I might have my request,
>   that God would grant what I hope for,
> That God would be willing to crush me,
>   to let loose his hand and cut me off!
> Then I would still have this consolation —
>   my joy in unrelenting pain —
>   that I had not denied the words of the Holy One.
>   -Job 6:8-10 (NIV)

Before discussing the nature of the book of Job itself, I want to tell you the story of another Job syndrome, the excruciatingly painful experience of Ron and Vicki.[6] Ron and Vicki are presently semi-retired, having served as missionaries to Ghana, Africa, where they have devoted their time to build churches, dig wells, assist orphanages, mentor and encourage pastors, and to minister in numerous other ways to advance the cause of Christ and the Gospel.

Ron and Vicki's lives were changed forever on an otherwise normal Sunday morning, June 6, 1982. Ron was dressed for church in a suit and tie, and he was calling for the children to get dressed, also. Vicki had a job as housekeeping assistant at a large hotel. She was working that Sunday and wasn't in the house. They were the blessed parents of four wonderful children, of which the second-oldest child was Michael. The other children reported that Michael was not home. Ron asked where he was, and they told him Michael had gone with Ron's nephew Eddie. Ron and his brother, David, worked together in a contracting business and, also owned a turf farm. Michael had gone with his cousin Eddie to mow in a field of grass. Because of heavy rains, they were behind in keeping the grass mowed, so they were mowing 24 hours per day. The mowing was being done by bush hogs that were fourteen feet wide pulled by large tractors.

About the time, Ron was trying to locate Michael, he received a phone call from his brother, who lived fifteen minutes away at the time. David called to tell Ron there had been an accident. David did not want to tell the details, but Ron insisted he tell. Michael had been on the fender of the tractor. The boys had been told that they were not to ride the tractor on the big square fenders, but sometimes boys just aren't as obedient as we wish they would be. When they got to the back side of the field, there were limbs overhanging the edge of the field. They are not certain, but they believed that a limb caught Michael and threw him behind the tractor into the bush hog. He was killed instantly.

Vicki was contacted by her sister-in-law, Mary, David's wife. Mary came to where Vicki was working and told her there had been an accident. From the limited description, Vicki said that she was thinking of some cuts or broken bones. Mary then said that it was serious. Vicki asked, "How bad is it?" Mary still did not tell her of the death of her son, Michael. Vicki was thinking about insurance cards and other possible needs on the way to the field. Driving to the field, they met three ambulances, which were having difficulty finding the site. Upon arriving, Vicki saw Ron's car in the field and wanted to go there to him. She said, "Something inside of me said, 'You can't handle it—what you would see,' and I knew that was the Holy Spirit." David then came up to the car window and told Vicki that Michael was dead. She exclaimed, "Don't joke with me; that's not funny!" She did not want to believe what he was saying.

Vicki said, "Then the pain starts!" She described that many people want to know what kind of pain one goes through when you find out about your own child's death. She said her best description is, "It is like hard labor. Part of you is tearing up inside. You can't breathe. You feel like you are giving birth—exactly like hard labor." Vicki's experience sheds real insight into the part of the curse in Genesis 3:16 on women, "Unto the woman he said, I will greatly multiply thy sorrow and thy conception; in sorrow thou shalt bring forth children…" Vicki had hard labor bringing Michael into the world, and hard labor letting him go.

The complex emotions of such an event were devastating. David was laying down in the back seat and was heaving in grief. A little later Ron met David, and they comforted each other in an embrace. Vicki described it as "probably one of the greatest signs of love I've ever seen...Ron showed love to David even though Michael, his own son, was now dead...he loved David, too." To this day, these men love each other as well as their other brothers. It has always been a tight knit family.

Ron recalled the phone call from David telling him about the accident. He said his first reaction was anger. It was not "anger at persons" but an overwhelming anger that he had a problem. He related, "I believe that man always tries to blame God...because God could have stopped the machine...God could have made the day another day." In pain, like Ron was experiencing, we always think of the "could have" or "should have" scenarios. There were other details of this story such as the gruesomeness of the condition of Michael's body, but as the book of Job spared the details of Job's calamities, I will spare the details about Michael.

When talking about the dynamics of their reaction to this horrible situation, Ron summed it up saying, "It makes you come to places in your life where you ask yourself, 'Why?'" That is the most perplexing question we all have in times of extreme pain. As Ron's and Vicki's experiences certainly teach us, there is no simple answer to that question. The various and complex paths to understanding the contributing factors of the answer to that question is the real reason for this writing.

In the interview with Ron and Vicki, I asked, "What

was your greatest pain?" Here are the responses. Vicki related that it was finding out how he died. "As a mother, you want to take the pain for them." Then she quickly added, "I really felt God there the whole time." Ron related that for him it would be "the pain of the accident—the knowing." With a very serious expression and a somber tone, he continued, "The scene—every dead animal I would pass on the road, roadkill as we call it, would bring back the scene to me for a long time." He explained that you cannot go through something like this with someone so close without it doing something to you, "and then how to live afterwards, because it's almost like now you have a **limp in your life not by your choice**—you carry it like a sickness." Vicki enjoined, "Your motivation is gone." Then Ron said, "I still had many jobs I was under contract to perform, but I had lost the heart to do it…it brings you to a place where you realize God is your answer; He's your healer; He's your strength."

Jacob, the patriarch, walked with a limp in his life. After the years of working with his father-in-law, Laban, Jacob received an order from God to return to his homeland. The difficulty with that was his extremely problematic relationship with his brother, Esau. Jacob had left home fleeing from revenge-bound Esau who wanted to kill him. As Jacob entered the land, he sent a great present to Esau by his servants announcing that Jacob would soon follow. There had been many significant turns in Jacob's life, but the evening before he met Esau was life changing. In Genesis 32:1-32, especially Verses 25-32, we have the story of Jacob's God-encounter. Jacob was visited by God in human form (a theophany). Recognizing that this was his only hope for salvation, Jacob held on to the Man and wrestled with Him until almost daybreak saying, "I will not let thee go, except thou bless me." (Verse 26) **Too many fail to recognize this important truth: the next event in this story is in fact an act of God! God gave Jacob a limp for the rest of his life** by shortening the sinew of his hip joint as He "touched the hollow of his thigh; and the hollow of Jacob's thigh was out of joint." (Verse 25) **Jacob was changed forever by a physical handicap! His name was also changed from Jacob, heel-catcher or supplanter (con man), to Israel, prince or ruler of God. When God decides to do a make-over in our lives, no matter how painful, we need to embrace it in worship and thanksgiving.** In Jacob's case, walking with a limp, "and he halted upon his thigh," (Verse 31) was, in reality, a true blessing from God. As with Jacob, so it was with Ron and Vicki; they were learning to walk with their limp.

Ron related his experience later in the evening the day of the accident. He said, "I honestly didn't know how I was going to sleep...I wondered how I could shut my eyes." He explained that in shutting his eyes he could only see the scene of the accident. Family members were coming in from all over. Several of Ron's brothers had come. Ron continued, "You know? When things are going great for you, everybody's happy, but when things happen tragically to you, your happiness is tried." What a unique way of expressing the pressure and pain!

Ron explained that he was so exhausted that he had to try to rest. He said, "When I shut my eyes, I saw something I had never seen before…I saw like a large waterfall, and I saw colors, bright colors, individual colors like blue, silver, gold and green—all these colors in this waterfall except they were individual, and they all sparkled…so brilliant like no color on earth…kind of like a rainbow…God gave this to me." This vision gave Ron a peace, so that he could sleep. When he got up the next morning, he told the family what he saw. One of his brothers reminded him that there are references in the Bible, which refer to God giving peace in times of trouble.

> Peace I leave with you, my peace I give unto you: not as the world giveth, give I unto you. Let not your heart be troubled, neither let it be afraid.
> -John 14:27

> And the peace of God, which passeth all understanding, shall keep your hearts and minds through Christ Jesus.
> -Philippians 4:7

> Now the Lord of peace himself give you peace always by all means…
> -2 Thessalonians 3:16a

I asked about whether fear was a part of their reaction to the tragedy. Vicki related that from the time of the accident she had not driven for weeks. When she drove for the first time in over a month, *the Satan*, the Accuser, (the same spiritual enemy as in Job chapter one) attempted to strike fear in her heart. She told this story, "The devil came at me...he came at me with this, 'You don't know that Mike is in heaven. He could have gone to hell. He was not perfect.'" The kind of fear she was experiencing was not for her or family. It was the fear that Mike was not in heaven. To her mother's heart, that was an extreme pain. She began to rebuke those thoughts and to pray that God would make the doubt and pain go away. Vicki recalled having heard a lady television evangelist say, "When the Devil comes at you so strong, start singing praises to the Lord." As Vicki began singing praises, she relaxed and began to feel the peace of God.

Ron said that he did not have any fear. We discussed the fact that the vision Ron had of the waterfall colors continued to have the effect of peace in his life. He agreed saying, "To this day, I always see it."

I asked the question, "After all these years, have you ever discovered why you had this trial?" Vicki said, "The only thing I've thought about is God knew how we would deal with it. He chose us to go through it. If it was an attack from *Satan*, I don't know. I truly believe that God is in control. You either believe it, or you don't." Ron made this perceptive observation, **"Even if you go the route that you're under attack, still God's in control."**

We talked about the fact that most people who experience the Job syndrome are not able to tell you why. Very few discover the answer to that question. Ron said, "It's not something that you lay in bed and decide, 'This is your direction.'" **With most of us, it is a day to day gentle and subtle leading of the Holy Spirit. In the Job syndrome, one is most often not aware of that leading until much later.**

Vicki reflected on the day of the accident. She recalled telling God she loved Michael so much as a mother, "…and I remember God speaking to me through the Holy Spirit, 'I loved him more as a Father!' That brought a peace; as much as I loved him, God loved him more."

As we continued to talk, Ron revealed his attachment to Job. He said, "When we went through this with Michael, the loss of Michael, I read Job very well and re-read Job more than once, maybe four or five times…God didn't give up on Job. It was a plan, and God knows who He can display…so He can get the glory."

Ron went on to talk about how their Job syndrome affected their lives, "Out of the accident, we became even more committed to God…you either become better, or you become bitter." Vicki added, **"There's a feeling that I went through. I don't understand it myself, but I felt honored that God would choose us."** Knowing these faithful and committed people, I believe that they were truly "honored" to be chosen by our heavenly Father just as Job was chosen.

Another question I asked was, "Did you have or experience a Job-like revelation of God when He showed up and talked to you?" For Vicki, it was in the inspired words of the Holy Spirit at critical times of emotional need. The scriptures came alive. For Ron, it was a process. He said, "I went through five months of depression." Later he continued, "I remember when God spoke to me…it wasn't a voice; it was a knowing in my spirit. He said, 'Go to lunch but only take someone with you that can lift you.'" During that time, he continued to work the contracts they had but with emotional stress. The crew took their lunch hour about one o'clock each day. Ron knew immediately who that should be. He asked a younger man who was a recently converted Christian to join him. As their daily lunches were enjoyed, their conversations about God, the things of God, and living the true Christian life began to show Ron that he had much to share. He was constantly encouraging the young man, and **that ministry began to encourage Ron himself. God was in the ministry!**

As Ron and Vicki went through a fiery trial that would have brought many to despair and ultimately to defeat, they purposed not to give up on God. In a similar way, our hero, Job, was brought face to face with the temptation to surrender his faith and to "curse God, and die" (Job 2:9). **Surrender to the will of *the Satan* is never a realistic option. The caring and all-wise God Who allowed the trials and performed the victories for Job, and for Ron and Vicki, is the same God Who is working in us.** We must never forget that with God "there is no respect of persons."

> For there is no respect of persons with God.
> -Romans 2:11

Knowing that whatsoever good thing any man doeth, the same shall he receive of the Lord, whether he be bond or free. And, ye masters, do the same things unto them, forbearing threatening: knowing that your Master also is in heaven; neither is there respect of persons with him.

-Ephesians 6:8-9

And if ye call on the Father, who without respect of persons judgeth according to every man's work, pass the time of your sojourning here in fear: Forasmuch as ye know that ye were not redeemed with corruptible things, as silver and gold…

-1 Peter 1:17-18a

What our Father has done for Ron, Vicki, and Job, He will do for any faithful worshiper. Trust Him immediately! Trust Him completely! Trust Him ultimately!

I will now turn to an overview of the book of Job, which will give a foundational background for the spiritual concepts for the entirety of this writing. Job's story is profound at many levels and its truth is revelation to the life of every believer who, in suffering, needs comfort and encouragement. Whether one is experiencing a Job syndrome or trying to encourage another person in suffering, we may constantly learn from Job's example and the wisdom expressed in this marvelous book.

Structure, Location and Characters of Job

In order to grasp the extreme dynamics of Job's

suffering and restoration, it is important to establish the book of Job as a part of the inspired Holy Bible. That statement at first may seem unnecessary to most readers who accept the Bible, as a whole, to be God's inspired Word. Yet, for many decades in liberal theological circles, there have been strong and powerful attempts to disallow parts of the Scripture, such as Job, which are considered inauthentic. We will need to understand the book's uniqueness and its historical impact in both the Jewish and Christian worlds. Jew and Christian alike identify with Job's need to cry out to God as in the passage seen at the beginning of this chapter. This book, as no other book of the Bible, speaks to our own very personal suffering and the desire for deliverance from it.

The book of Job may be the most influential and best known of the sixty-six books of the Bible outside the spheres of the Christian and Jewish communities. Writers, composers, and artists whose work in the fields of literature, music, dance, and art have taken material directly from Job or utilized significant parts of Job's story. Almost all commentators and writers who have written about Job speak extravagantly with admiration and praise for this extraordinary book. Because of its literary greatness among other characteristics, one of the preeminent Jewish scholars of the past century, Robert Gordis, claimed the book to have "universal appeal."[7] With obvious admiration, another commentator, J. E. Smith, stated that few compositions match the mental and emotional power of Job. Almost poetically Smith stated, "One who has eavesdropped on the discussions in the heavenly court, visited Job at the city dump, weighed the arguments of Job and his friends, and cowered before the thundering barrage of questions from the God of the Whirlwind can never be the same again."[8]

The book of Job is certainly a marvel of literary expertise. It is easy to recognize three basic divisions generally described as prologue, dialogue, and epilogue. This is the classic A-B-A form that is similar to the musical form of statement of a theme, development, and recapitulation. I, personally, have often admired Beethoven's *Fifth Symphony*, especially the first movement, which so emotionally exhibits this timeless form in the famous theme described as fate's rap at the door, ta, ta, ta, taah. In Job, this form can also be described as introduction, argument, and conclusion.

There is a great deal of parallel structure to the book, which could be seen as a literary expansion of the general form of the Hebrew poetry known as parallelism. The vast majority of the book of Job is in Hebrew poetry. Actually, almost all of chapters 3-41 exhibit this form of literature. Hebrew poetry does not have rhyme or rhythm, as we would expect in most English poetry. What makes Hebrew poetry is a parallelism of thought. A statement is made, and then another statement is made that has a direct correlation with the first statement. Occasionally, a third or even a fourth statement will be added, which are also connected to the original statement in a similar fashion. The additional statement or statements can be connected in English translation with such words as "and," "also," "furthermore," or "even" so that the effect is further explanation or restatement of the original thought. Sometimes the second statements are contrasting or negative and may use connecting words such as "but," "however," "then," "except," and words similar. Even when the connecting words are not used in the Hebrew or in the translation, they can be read into the verses without doing damage to the meaning. The following are examples from Job, Psalms, and Proverbs of the parallelism of Hebrew poetry. (Connecting words in parenthesis are mine, which are added for illustration.)

Job 28:12-13, where Job is describing wisdom:

But where can wisdom be found?
    And where is the place of understanding?
Man does not know its value,
    Nor is it found in the land of the living.

                                      (NASB)

Psalm 51:3-4, when David confessed his sin:

For I know my transgressions,
    And my sin is ever before me.
Against You, You only, I have sinned
      And done what is evil in Your sight,
      So that You are justified when You speak
      And blameless when You judge.

                                      (NASB)

Proverbs 8:17-21, where Wisdom as a person speaks:

> I love those who love me;
>> And those who diligently seek me will find me.
> Riches and honor are with me,
>> (Even) Enduring wealth and righteousness.
> My fruit is better than gold, even pure gold,
>> And my yield better than choicest silver.
> I walk in the way of righteousness,
>> (And) In the midst of the paths of justice,
> To endow those who love me with wealth,
>> That I may fill their treasuries.
>
>> (NASB)

When studied, particularly in a good modern translation such as the New American Standard Bible Updated Edition seen above, this Hebrew parallelism has a beautiful flow to the reading and a powerful impact on the meaning of the message. There are many passages in the Old Testament, which utilize this form of literature. This is not easily seen in the King James Version, which by the way, is the premier English version, but as it is printed, there is no indication of the poetic parallelism. The New King James Version does rectify this oversight and does a good job of showing the parallelism. These poetic passages can be found in the Pentateuch, a few places in the historical books, all of the poetic books, and often in the prophets.

There is a distinct build-up of tension in the various sections of the book of Job. This tension increase is seen as the speeches of the dialogue move toward the climatic interruption by God. The second confrontation of *the Satan* and God was more drastic than the first. In the theophany

(God's appearance in the whirlwind), *Yahweh's* second address to Job was more profound than the first. God's two talks with Job were far more important to the meaning of the book than His two talks with *the Satan* at the beginning. These illustrations are only a few of the structural parallels, which have great drama and literary impact. They also should be recognized as commanding arguments for the planning of a single author, for the integrity of the book, and for the unity of the writing. Once again, this is dramatic evidence of the inspiration of the Holy Spirit in the writing of this incredibly cohesive book. As Christian believers, we must hold tenaciously to the truth that "All Scripture is inspired by God and profitable for teaching, for reproof, for correction, for training in righteousness…" (2 Timothy 3:16, NASB)

The story of Job followed the tripartite pattern noted above. **Job's life lived in *shalom* (peace and prosperity), regressed into *rah* (evil as in calamity and affliction), and then progressed into even greater *shalom* than before.** This is the part of Job's life story that took forty-two chapters of scripture to tell. With such perfect structure and such a powerful story so obviously inspired by the Holy Spirit, there must be great revelations of truth in this book for all peoples, everywhere, for all time. **We may learn from this book that our covenant-keeping God, *Yahweh*, always sees, cares, and ultimately responds, and that we should trust Him implicitly.**

The narrative began by introducing Job, a man living in the land of Uz. The Hebrew linguists are divided on the meaning of the name *Job*. The most often espoused meaning is derived from a root, which translates "to be hostile."[9] Interpretation of this root follows two paths: (1) it means to be hated or persecuted, and (2) it means an adversary or hater (implying a hater of God).[10] Another translation path followed by some is that of a root meaning to be "'strong', 'brave', 'warlike'."[11] A third meaning of the name *Job* is in a derivative of an Arabic root interpreted as "to return," or "to be converted."[12] There are other speculations, but the effect of that diversity of opinion is that the true meaning of Job's name cannot be ascertained confidently. Because of the nature of the story and the essence of its meaning, I lean heavily towards the interpretation that the name *Job* indicates he is the object of hostility and persecution. After all, it is obvious to all who read his story that Job is both hated and persecuted by *the Satan* who did not hesitate to go to the full limits, which God placed on Job's trials.

The placement of the Land of Uz holds a similar ambiguity as that of the name *Job*. The most heavily supported location connects Uz with Edom as in Jeremiah 25:20. Here is given a list of kingdoms south, southwest and southeast of Israel. This connection is also seen in Lamentations 4:21, "Rejoice and be glad, O daughter of Edom, that dwellest in the land of Uz…" This would place Uz south to southeast of the Dead Sea and south of Moab. Other interpreters associate Uz with Aram, a location to the northeast of the Sea of Galilee. Like the meaning of the name *Job*, the location of Uz remains a matter of debate. As

I connect the dots of Old Testament information on this geographical location, I hold the opinion that Uz was a place in or near Edom and was in what is presently the nation of Jordan. This location fits with the traditional rabbinic teaching that Moses is the author of the book. It is in close proximity to Midian where Moses spent forty years of his life. Midian is south and southwest of Edom on the east of the Gulf of Aqaba. Having this proximity to Edom would certainly make the story of the great man from Uz available to Moses in the land of Midian.

The author gave a description of Job in the first verse of the book that would be repeated two more times by God Himself, "This man was perfect and upright, fearing Elohim and turning away from evil" (Dhorme).[13] **This three times stated assessment of Job's character (Job 1:1; 1:8; 2:3) is an absolutely necessary element to the purpose of this writing and for solutions to the Job syndrome.** Since this will be discussed in detail below, a brief comment is sufficient here. Job was unquestionably a righteous man both validated and venerated by God Himself. God declared, "There is no one like him on the earth" (v. 8, Dhorme).[14] It was to such a man that unimaginable tragedy would soon come.

After a succinct portrayal of Job's family and his wealth (1:2-5), a scene in the courts of heaven showed the presence of the sons of *Elohim*, the angels, as they presented themselves for the purpose of giving accounts of their activities. Among them was *the Satan* who entered into dialogue with God. The Hebrew is *ha Satan*, which means "the adversary at law," or "the prosecutor" (Dhorme).[15] *The Satan* then is the Accuser—he does what his title indicates. God asked *the Satan* if he were aware of his "servant Job" (1:8), and he repeated the earlier description of Job as a perfect and upright man who reverenced God and shunned evil. *The Satan* responded in good rhetorical style with his own question, **"Doth Job fear God for naught?"** (1:9).

Here, in this question about Job's motivation for serving God, is the challenge of the entire book. Was Job's piety pure? Was it totally unselfish? Was it for "naught?" Was it for no reason? Or, did he serve God for the blessings and prosperity? Did Job himself live inside the box of the doctrine of retribution with all its limitations or outside that box in exquisite freedom in direct relationship to *Yahweh*? **Job's motivation for serving God was the beyond-human question. It was the cosmic question then as it is still, yet that question could only be answered on earth in Job's life,** as it must be answered in the existential "living out" of the faith of every believer. **Do we serve God for "naught?" This question gets to the heart of the Job syndrome. The trial is always a sifting, a shaking out of our motivations which refine our faith. We are challenged as was Job to determine if we serve God for the benefits or for "naught."**

It seems utterly incredible, but God accepted as valid the challenge of the accuser. A test of Job's integrity and loyalty to God would be allowed, but it could not include touching Job personally (1:10-12). **Giving His permission to *the Satan* to test Job, God also placed a limitation as**

to how far that test could go. Job's whole identity and destiny in society was at stake. The calamities began to decrease disastrously Job's things and family (1:13-19). In quick succession, four tragedies befell Job and were reported, all in one day, within minutes of each other. Two of these losses (the first and third) were due to criminal acts of evil men under satanic influence. The other two (the second and fourth) were so-called "acts of God" produced supernaturally by *the Satan* himself. **The source of trial then may come from the acts of men or from the devil and his demonic forces.** The sequence of Job's losses is also significant: (1) the loss of oxen and asses along with the attending servants took Job's means of farming and sustaining life as these animals were the John Deere and Kubota tractors of Job's time; (2) the loss of his flocks and shepherds by fire took his major source of food and trade ("sheep" here represent sheep and goats); (3) the theft of camels and murder of camel drivers took his ability to trade locally and internationally as camels were the trucking industry of Job's day; and (4) the deaths of his children in the tornado took the loves of his life and his Middle Eastern sense of self-worth.

Job's response to the satanic attacks was astounding! "Then Job arose, and rent his mantle, and shaved his head, and fell down upon the ground, and worshipped," (1:20). That is so profound as to make me want to sit in contemplative awe ... wow! Was that man super-human? At first glance, it would seem so, but within weeks, or possibly months, he was cursing his birthday and lamenting his excruciatingly painful existence. In this experience of Job is a great lesson to be learned. **An initial shock of tragedy is one kind of trial, but extended suffering is an entirely different level of trial.** Either of the events of loss Job suffered could have been dealt with individually had there been enough time, but Job did not have sufficient time to grieve and adjust from one great loss before he was brought to ruin in another and then another loss just as evil. **When nights and days merge into gray and neither sunrise nor sunset offers a hope to change for the better, one's faith is brought to the brink of utter darkness—total despair seems inevitable. The Job syndrome is at maximum effect!**

The next scene was another accounting of *the Satan* to God. In similar words as before God reminded *the Satan* of Job and taunted him by adding that Job had held his integrity. The Hebrew word translated "integrity" means completion in the sense of innocence. Job did not sin! He completely maintained his innocence before God, even after his wife taunted him to give up his innocence and to curse God and die. In total rejection of that idea, Job kept his integrity. Twice the writer says that Job did not sin, especially with his lips (Job 1:22; 2:10). It is not my argument to make with those who claim that Job sinned. There are two witnesses of Scripture that Job did not sin.

The Satan quickly retorted that a man would give up anything to save his own life. God responded by giving him permission for a personal physical attack (2:1-6), but again God placed a limitation that *the Satan* could not kill Job. Job was smitten with sore boils from his scalp to his soles. The word "sore" is the same word that is translated "evil" three times previously in chapters one and two (again the Hebrew word *rah* meaning *calamity* or *evil works*). Evil, the thing that Job had shunned, and from which he had steered others, was now afflicting his bones (2:5) and manifesting in excruciatingly painful disfiguring eruptions from his skin (2:7, 8, 12; 6:7; 7:5; 17:7; 19:20; 30:17, 18, 30). **The evil of calamity from without and the evil of affliction from within were testing Job to the limits of physical endurance, to the overload point of his emotional capacity, and to the foundation of his theological world-view.** Job is finally tempted by the admonition of his wife who uses the very words of *the Satan* that Job should "curse Elohim and die!" (Dhorme).[16]

The length of time Job remained in this diseased condition is unknown, but it was certainly more than a few days. His three friends from their respective foreign countries had time to receive the news, to meet together, and to travel (probably by camel train) to Job's locale in order to try to encourage him. It is truly remarkable that Job's friends went to such sacrifice and effort in order to help him in his time of awful calamity. After their arrival, they, Eliphaz the Temanite, Bildad the Shuhite and Zophar the Naamathite, along with Job, sat in the dust together in stark wordless mourning over Job's tragic condition for seven days. In the words of the author, the friends of Job "saw that his grief was very great." Anderson summarized that poignant scene beautifully:

Attention is focused, not on the abstract mystery of evil, not on the moral question of undeserved suffering, but on one man's physical existence in bodily pain. There was nothing to be said. These wise men are horrified and speechless. They were true friends, bringing to Job's lonely ash-heap the compassion of a silent presence.[17]

"Great" grief is the overwhelming emotion of one in the Job syndrome. Just as Job sat immobilized on the ash heap, convulsing in utter agony, trying to rid himself of the deep hurt seemingly squeezing the life out of him, so does everyone who is in a true Job syndrome. Job expressed it like this:

> God has made me a byword to everyone,
>   a man in whose face people spit.
> My eyes have grown dim with grief;
>   my whole frame is but a shadow.
>
>   -Job 17:6–7 (NIV)

I believe a real Job syndrome is not a one-day deal. It is when the pain and hurt keep rolling in like angry waves of the sea, day after day, after day, that we scream again and again, "I can't take anymore!" Then we realize we are in a full-blown Job syndrome. In Job's case, we don't know how long Job had been in his "great" grief before the arrival of the friends. It had been most likely weeks, if not months. Job made an insightful comment about the length of his suffering:

> Has not man a term of service on the earth?
>> And are not his days like the days of a hired worker?
> Like a slave who gasps for the shade,
>> and like a hired worker who hopes for his wages,
> Thus I have inherited months of emptiness,
>> and nights of misery are allotted to me.
> When I lie down, I wonder, "When shall I rise?"
>> During the length of the evening,
>> I am fed up with tossing until dawn.
> My flesh is clothed with worms and crusts;
>> my skin forms a scab and oozes.
> My days go past faster than a weaver's shuttle;
>> they are cut off as the end of a thread.
>
> —Job 7:1-6 (Hartley)

You see, Job indicates that his suffering had gone on for months, which at that time included the visit of the friends. What we do know for sure is that when the friends came, they spent seven whole days in silent empathetic grieving with Job.

This brings us to the marvelous and intriguing middle of the book (chapters 3-41) where the characters of the book speak their minds about God, life, nature, and Job's problems. Each of these wise men takes the stage to add his thoughts to the debate. They laud *Elohim*, the Creator, and *El Shaddai*, the Almighty. They are theologians and philosophers. Their logic seems indestructible. Yet, the three friends, Eliphaz, Bildad, and Zophar, failed in one major area. **Their otherwise brilliant view of God**

denied His utter sovereignty by restricting His ways to the boundaries of the laws of retribution. When the dialog between Job and his three friends winds down, we are introduced to Elihu who, like John the Baptist, is the forerunner of God. Elihu reaches new heights in describing God and His ways. It is then God appears to Job in the whirlwind and declares His sovereignty over all things, people, and events.

After a period of time and much dialogue, even debate, between the protagonist, Job, and the other speakers, Eliphaz, Bildad, Zophar, Elihu and God, the story is picked up in the epilogue (42:7-17) to conclude with a triumphant ending. At the command of God, Job acted as priest again (see 1:5 and 42:7-9) making a sacrifice and praying for his three friends. That event was the real turning point in Job's earthly destiny. God "...rehabilitated the position of Job, because he interceded for his friends, and Yahweh doubled all that had belonged to him," (42:10, Dhorme).[18] Job's doubled blessing included fourteen sons and three daughters. A particle of the numeral *sibanah* (translated "seven" in the King James Version) gives it a double seven meaning. So, Job's family is doubled what he had in the prologue as well as his goods and herds. Job was returned to his family and community much greater than at his beginning. His sons were many; his daughters were beautiful and given equality with their brothers (the first mention of the equality of women since the fall of Adam and Eve); and, Job was given long life observing his offspring to the fourth generation. Job's passing at the age of one hundred and forty carried a special epitaph, "So Job died, being old and full of days." (42:17) This is the same form of epitaph used for some of the greatest among God's servants, i.e., Abraham (Gen. 25:8), Isaac (Gen. 35:29), David (1 Chr. 29:28), and Jehoida the priest (2 Chr. 24:15).

We should not pass by lightly, overlook or otherwise diminish the vast majority of the book in the middle, between the beginning and the end of the story of Job's experience. It was here that Job responded in speeches and sets of speeches making up twenty chapters in the forty-two chapter book (the dialogue actually covers thirty-four chapters). The discourses of Job's three friends, Eliphaz, Bildad and Zophar, were interwoven with Job's speeches in a cyclical manner until the final speeches given by Elihu and God. The challenges and responses of these dialogues progressed in the details of accusations and in emotional tension until Job moved on to address God in a unilateral and legal style. He was pleading his case as though he were in the heavenly court before the Judge of all the earth. Job repeatedly asserted his innocence to his friends and to God. He ultimately insisted that God declare him *not guilty* or to vindicate him in the presence of his accusers. Incredibly, when God does speak to Job, He does neither of those things directly. God reveals certain things about Himself, which ultimately expands Job's spiritual horizon. Job sees God and quits looking at his own status and condition. In that revelation, Job worshipped!

This brief summary of the book of Job, an

extraordinary book telling a most dramatic and captivating story, reveals God's ways of dealing with us in the midst of our most extreme circumstances. As Job pressed through to his God encounter and then enjoyed the crowning blessing of God's approval, **we too may hold fast to an absolute confidence that our *Yahweh*, our covenant-keeping God, will indeed bring about our own deliverance.**

Literary Considerations

The book of Job contains many elements of fine literary form, and it exhibits characteristics of several genres. The prologue and epilogue of the book are prose and they are narratives. These are also straightforward biblical Hebrew with hardly any surprises. The dialogue portion (chapters 3-41) is quite another story. It is in Hebrew poetry with the exceptions of very brief introductions to the interlocutors, the speakers. The Hebrew of this section is much more difficult than the narratives. There are more *hapax legomena* (a one and only usage of a word in the entire Bible) than any other Old Testament book, and words which are found elsewhere in scripture only a few times are found throughout the book. Several of the different types of literature of the book of Job were listed by R. L. Alden as a "…treasure trove of word pictures, metaphors, similes, tightly reasoned logic, prayers, irony, insults, insinuations, protestations, exaggerations, fabrications, and interrogations."[19] With drama, intrigue, mystery, tragedy, philosophy, theology, relationships, and a theophany, the book of Job truly is one of a kind.

In critical theological circles, there is debate as to who authored the book of Job. That discussion is always tied to the similar dispute about the date of authorship. The dating covers a number of centuries from the time of Moses to as late as the second century B.C. It is admitted that the earlier rabbinic traditions did not question Mosaic authorship. Why is this information important in this discussion? It has a strong influence on one's belief that the book is the story of a real person and his experience rather than a fable.

Various arguments are given for later dating: (1) for dating during the time of Solomon, the parallels of Job with other Wisdom literature are used; (2) for exilic or post-exilic dating, a perceived parabolic association with the suffering nation of Judah under Babylonian captivity is seen; or (3) the similarities of certain passages of Isaiah are argued to have Job dependent on Isaiah rather than Isaiah dependent on Job. There are simple arguments, which cast doubt on these positions for later dating. First, although there are a few similarities of Job with other Wisdom writings, they are still very different in structure and style, and the old but very important question of who is quoting whom is applicable. Second, it is so very improbable that any writer, who would be writing a parable of Judah's woes, could go on for the length of Job without mentioning that connection in some form. Third, if indeed there are real quotations between Job and Isaiah (that is itself questionable), again, who is quoting whom?

Regardless of one's position on authorship and dating the book, it is agreed by all that the story of Job is set in the patriarchal period. There are several reasons. Job's wealth, like that of Abraham, Isaac, and Jacob, was measured in the numbers of livestock (cf. Job 1:3 and Gen. 26:13, 14). The currency used by Job was the *kesitah* (42:11), the same as in the time of Jacob (Gen. 33:19). Job, as the head of the family acted as priest (1:5; 42:8) as did the patriarchs. Like Abraham interceded for Abimelech (Gen. 20:7), Job interceded for Eliphaz, Bildad, and Zophar (42:8). Job was long lived, living to the age of one hundred and forty, as were the patriarchs. Finally, Job's epitaph, "So Job died, being old and full of days," (42:17) was in the same phrasing as that of Abraham (Gen. 25:8) and Isaac (Gen. 35:29).[20]

Some commentators see the book as a complete fabrication by an exilic or postexilic writer, so the patriarchal evidences mean nothing more than a setting for the allegory. Others believe that the story is based on some historical experience, but the book has greatly expanded the tale. Both of these positions make some assumptions, which are truly incredible. By placing the date of writing between the seventh and second centuries B.C., one has to believe that an oral story survived for well over a thousand years, or that the author had such unbelievable skill that he could authentically write in a Hebrew style of antiquity with little or no actual historical evidences to use as a guide.[21] The commentators who held to a later dating used several arguments. They did not feel that the sophistication of the conflict of suffering and retribution could have been conceived earlier. The theology in Job was seen as being too advanced for an earlier age. The nature of the Wisdom literature characteristics, although showing a few similarities with extra-biblical wisdom literature, did not reach its full development until the time of Solomon.

Each of these arguments, and numerous others, are based on an assumption that human understanding and intelligence have always been in an evolutionary process parallel to technological and scientific development. An exposure of the fallacy of such an assumption can be seen in a question of whether there are greater thinkers today than Socrates, Aristotle, Augustine, Aquinas, Shakespeare, de Vinci, and Bach. None of those gentlemen ever flushed a toilet, yet the world has been changed forever by their ability to think. It should not be assumed that Moses had any less ability to think or write in the language of his day than Solomon or Isaiah would have in their eras. Nor should anyone expect less of an earlier writer of Job than a later author. It should be obvious that I will stand by early rabbinic tradition and believe that Moses was the author of this astounding book. As indicated before, Moses certainly had the opportunity to be familiar with Job's story from being in close proximity to Uz, while living in Midian for forty years.

As we read the book of Job to be enlightened, encouraged, and strengthened for what lies ahead, we must base our faith on its long held acceptance as a part of the canon of the Scripture, and that it was inspired by the direct action of the Holy Spirit. It is a real story of a real man in a real-world circumstance. This book, in ways unlike any other book of the Bible, speaks to each suffering believer with authority about God's ultimate sovereignty and care.

The Purpose of the Book of Job

Those who write about the book of Job seem to have strong individual concepts as to the purpose of the book. Perhaps the seemingly vague and unfocused characteristic of not having a clearly discernable purpose is actually one of the book's greatest strengths. This must be so, because the book carries the ability to speak to every person at whatever stage of development he or she has reached in the Job syndrome. After noting the vast differences of opinion on the purpose and place of the book, one only has to read the book as he or she works through personal suffering to come to a realization of the encouragement, which comes from an identity with Job and his example.

Robert Gordis took a position on the goal and purpose of the book of Job that is far nobler than most other writers. Coming from his background as a Jewish professor in a major Hebrew university, Professor Gordis had few peers in the Hebrew language. He recognized in the author of Job a person of fine intellect, a deep emotional nature and a capacity for involvement with others. Although he argued for a much later date for the book, Gordis still addressed the effort of the writer of Job with much admiration when he wrote:

The result was a work of grand proportions, the writing of which probably spanned his lifetime. He attempted to grapple with the crucial questions with which the psalmist, prophet, and poet alike had wrestled for centuries and which remain the greatest stumbling blocks to religious faith: why do the wicked prosper and the righteous suffer? Why is there evil in a world created by a just God?[22]

Out of the numerous verses in Job, one thousand and seventy to be exact, not one, or even several of them, attempt to answer the questions posed by Gordis and the thousands, or millions, throughout history. There are answers in the book, but they are hidden in the stuff. Those who have gone before me in writing about Job have recognized the extreme complexity of expressing the goal or the purpose of the book. There are not a few; there are many paradoxes. There are not three or four; there are numerous ambiguities. Yet, the book with that noble story remains before us inspired by the Holy Spirit, God's chosen paradigm for believing sufferers.

The purpose of the book of Job is too multifaceted to state simply or precisely. It may be said that the purpose of Job is involved with offering a paradigm of a progressive development of spiritual maturity in direct relationship with God. This is a process, which will only be realized by faithfulness through adversity or suffering. In other words, **the Holy Spirit put the book of Job in the Bible so that we may identify with Job when we go through symptoms of his syndrome and be encouraged that**

God will ultimately bring about a triumphant outcome for us as we continue in a faithful relationship with Him.

MY PRAYER

My Father, I believe You inspired the book of Job for my personal education, encouragement and edification. Please prepare my heart and the hearts of my readers to receive the truth that You have hidden in the stuff of Job's life. I want to learn to be faithful to You no matter what—just like Job.

3
EVIDENCES OF THE JOB SYNDROME

> And now my life ebbs away;
> > days of suffering grip me.
> Night pierces my bones;
> > my gnawing pains never rest.
> In his great power [God] becomes like clothing to me;
> > he binds me like the neck of my garment.
> He throws me into the mud,
> > and I am reduced to dust and ashes.
> I cry out to you, O God, but you do not answer;
> > I stand up, but you merely look at me.
> You turn on me ruthlessly;
> > with the might of your hand you attack me.
> > > -Job 30:16-21 (NIV)

I heard the phone, but I could not get to it at that moment. When I picked it up, I saw that it was my brother, Troy. Being busy, I thought I would listen to the message in a few minutes and get back with him. Before that happened, another phone call came from Troy's son, Timothy, "Uncle Johnny, please pray. Dad's had a wreck and they are airlifting him to the nearest trauma unit fifty miles away." I had heard the helicopter lift off from the pad near my house and wondered who needed the emergency service. Pastor Tim had described how Troy had hit a tree head on. The tree was in a place where the road split into two lanes on either side of it. I began to pray and quickly got ready. My wife and I rushed to the sight. The wrecker was just pulling away with Troy's vehicle. The helicopter was already in route to the hospital.

We went back home and prepared to go to the big city hospital. The trip would take approximately an hour and twenty minutes. As I drove to the hospital, my mind was flooded with so many thoughts. Why didn't I rush to answer the phone? Why did this have to happen to Troy? Is he going to survive? How bad is he hurt? Will he be permanently disabled? WILL THE ATTACKS NEVER STOP? You see, Troy had suffered a heart attack a little over a year before the wreck. That event had left him with a very weak heart only functioning at about fifteen to twenty percent capacity.

Arriving at the hospital, I found out that Troy was critical. They had not determined if he had internal injuries. An imaging test had determined that from the airbag in the vehicle, Troy had suffered multiple fractures of bones in his facial mask. Amazingly, all the bones were in place and would require no surgery. The real danger was the expected swelling in his face and head. When further tests were done, the doctors reported there were no internal injuries. As hundreds of people were praying, we still did not see an instantaneous miracle; we did, however, welcome with thankfulness the quicker than expected reduction of swelling and the step-by-step progression of Troy's recovery.

This event was just one of several major trials Troy had over the last years of his life. His life was one wholly given to ministry in obedience to the command and call of Jesus from his early twenties. Having been a successful evangelist even making tours into faraway lands such as India, Philippines, Africa and the Caribbean, Troy guided a church as pastor into significant transitions, which greatly enhanced worship and ministry in the area over more than two decades. When the church was exploding with growth and activity, Troy's personal trials began. He lost a minister of music. Building program burdens began. A major transition from the former denomination into a vibrant nondenominational ministry was made. Shortly after that transition, the first major physical trial began. Troy suffered a stroke. That left a partial paralysis in the left side of his face and his left hand and fingers. Since he was also a gifted pianist, this had an emotional impact. The paralysis of the face stopped his ability to play the trumpet, because he could not form the embouchure necessary to play. The trumpet was a lifelong love. This facial paralysis was also a constant reminder of the stroke since often he would bite his jaw or tongue when trying to eat.

Several years later, on a mission trip to the Navajo nation in New Mexico, the second major physical attack happened. Troy suffered a heart attack, which drastically curtailed his activities because of the weak heart function. He entered a program, which prepared him for a heart transplant. He qualified, but he just could not bring himself to sign the final authorizations. Troy's battle with this decision is best described in the words of his wife, Terry:

> …that (the heart attack) began a drastic physical decline. His doctor had diagnosed bronchitis. However, when his symptoms were related to the cardiologist's nurse, she slammed her hand down on the clipboard and said, "How many times have I heard that!" His condition was such that he was immediately admitted to the hospital, and the many transplant tests began even though we had no idea that was the ultimate plan of action. Later Troy told the cardiologist that he would agree to a transplant, but before he left the office, he knew he should not have said, "Yes." We walked next door to the hospital for a test of some kind, and on the way back to our car in front of the cardiologist's office, we were debating whether or not we should go back up to tell him that Troy could not agree to the transplant after all. And to our surprise, walking along directly behind us, was the doctor's assistant. She heard our distress and asked us to sit down right there on a bench to talk. Troy explained to her that his faith would not allow a transplant. He said, "This goes against everything I have believed all my life." She assured him, his decision was okay and that the doctor would continue to treat him. We walked away that day relieved and feeling at peace that we had made the right decision for us.

During the time of the transplant program while Troy was wearing intravenous medications 24/7, the third physical trial occurred. The traumatic and excruciatingly painful wreck described above brought Troy to a new low physically and emotionally. The full-blown "trial of...faith" of 1 Peter 1:7 was testing my brother to the breaking point, but he never broke! After many hospitalizations and near-death experiences, Troy left us for a better home with our Lord in August of 2011. All who knew him well recognized the extreme nature of Troy's testing. His deeply held faith in God and his love for the calling and ministry are contemporary examples of faithfulness in trial. I truly marvel at the tenacity to purpose and the consecration to utter worship of his Lord, which exuded from his crushed life.

In order to describe Troy's Job syndrome, I want to quote a part of my address at his memorial service:

> In 1997 at a campmeeting, an internationally known television evangelist in a very rare moment for him, stopped in the middle of a message and walked toward Troy and gave him this personal prophecy, "You are a wet water walker." He went on to say the most significant thing related to the last several years of Troy's life, "All of your pinions will be stripped away." The significance of that statement can only be seen in relation to verse 4 of Psalm 91, "He will cover you with His pinions, And under His wings you may seek refuge." (NASB) Here is the interpretation of the prophecy and its fulfillment in Troy's life.
>
> My brother sailed on a crest of success for a lot of years as an evangelist and then as a pastor.

Beyond the comprehension of many who did not see the spiritual motivations in Troy, he followed the prompting and leading of the Holy Spirit to separate himself from our former denomination to start a new work as the Potter's House. A few of us came to realize that was only one step in his becoming the bishop, mentor, and spiritual father to many of you who sit here today as well as a number of congregations. His ministerial vision and influence these past twelve years far eclipsed his earlier ministry, for it was not just about the city and the tri-county area, or the big church. His bishopric covered several congregations in Florida, a number in other states and into foreign nations. In addition, Troy was highly honored with a Doctor of Divinity degree from Beacon University. I was so proud of that for him.

While his apostleship literally touched thousands, the prophecy began to come true in different strippings of the pinions. The dictionary definition of pinions is the outer edge of the wing of a bird containing the primary feathers. Pinions then are the strong feathers, which make flight possible. It should be obvious to all who knew Troy well that this eagle certainly went through his molting. In these past four years, our eagle landed. He graciously stepped aside to promote the ministry of his son, Timothy, the pastor of this church. Soon after that, the physical attacks of the enemy began to strip more of the pinions. Before those events, there was a baseless legal attack, which brought a degree of humiliation in this community which Troy gracefully lived down by exhibiting the most Christ-like forgiveness. In December of 2002, he began to experience the physical stripping. In Tampa with me and my son, Gabriel, while picking up the screen for the video, which you see here, my brother experienced his first stroke…

Two years ago, a heart attack killed the lower left lobe of his heart and the physical stripping intensified dramatically. Let it suffice here to say that it was so very painful to see the debilitating effect, especially since April of this year. In addition to his immediate family, I, along with my other brother Lemuel and our sister Alethea, walked that path with him. Father privileged me to suffer a similar condition so I could truly empathize with my brother. I will never forget the day as I was driving him on an errand; we talked of his trial and the evangelist's prophecy. He said with tears but not defeat, "John, I have been stripped of everything." Still, together we fought and commanded the spirits of affliction for each other. Yet my friends, let me shout, "There were many victories!" But, they were often private. Some may be thinking, "Brother John, why are you giving these sad details of his last years?" I have drawn you a picture so that you may know the magnitude of his victory.

In his molting period, my brother had a walk with God that few achieve. He learned to abide under the shadow of the pinions of the Almighty. The grounded molting eagle on the outside, on the inside began to grow a new beak and a new coat of feathers, particularly the pinions. At approximately 1:30 in the afternoon last Friday, our Eagle set his eye on the Son of God and took a flight heavenward where he presently soars in the very presence of God. Now, we all must follow him![23]

Troy went through an extended period of struggle with his health, which bears a striking similarity to Job's lengthy trial. The day after day suffering with debilitating weakness would have driven many if not most to defeat and giving up on the very idea of faith in God. Troy never gave up! Rather, he talked privately of his own "whirlwind" experiences of God's closeness and revelations. For example, during one of his hospitalizations, his blood pressure was dropping significantly, and it appeared he was dying. A nursing specialist was called to try to get the blood pressure back up. With all of us praying constantly, finally, after what seemed a forever, the pressure rose a few points at the time until it reached a non-critical point. Later, Troy told us that during this event, he saw his Lord, Jesus, standing in the corner of the hospital room just looking at him with the most calming and peaceful countenance.

Troy and I often talked about my study of Job. He encouraged me to write this book saying, "This message is really needed in the Church at large for this time." As I observed and participated vicariously in Troy's suffering, many of the insights and revelations given here were brought to fruition. So, now I will walk you through Job's story.

Background and Worldview of Job

What little is known of Job's background is given in the first five verses of the book. Job's name and the place name of his country were discussed above with inconclusive results. Job was not in any way identified with

God's covenant people Israel, yet he enjoyed an extraordinary, even unique, relationship with God similar to that of Israel's patriarchs. He was a worshipper, familiar with and wholly worshiping the God of creation.

Job's concept of Who God really is was foundational to his faith. We can see the meaning of that statement by looking at the use of the names of God in the book. In the prologue (1:1-2:13) of the book, the first name of God is *Elohim* Who is the Creator, the supreme God. This is the most common name for the Deity in the book of Job. The second name of God, which appears, is *Yahweh*. This name is translated "LORD" in the Authorized Version. *Yahweh* means the existent One Who is the God of covenant. In the dialogue (3:1-37:24), the names used by Job and his friends are *El*, *Eloah* and *Elohim*. *El* and *Eloah* are alternate forms of *Elohim*. Another name used in the dialogue is *Shaddai*.[24] *Shaddai* is often used in Job, and it means the Almighty One. In particular, this name recognizes the omnipotent power of God. (These names of God in the book of Job will be explained and expanded below in Chapter 4.)

Yahweh became known to Job in a new way in the theophany and epilogue (38:1- 42:12). Job's longing, before and during his trial, to know God personally was fulfilled and sealed in a relationship with *Yahweh*, the God of covenant. Job's understanding of God from the beginning was surely as rich and full as that of Abraham, Isaac, and Jacob, but, given its setting in patriarchal times, it was a pre-Mosaic, and therefore, a pre-Law understanding of

God and His ways. It is important to understand that Job's theology was basically the same as that of the patriarchs. He did not have the books of the law, the Pentateuch, as a foundation for his concepts of God and His ways. Like the patriarchs, Job's understanding of God had been passed down by word of mouth to each succeeding generation from Adam and Seth.

At the outset of his story, Job's world was comfortable, and his worldview was theistic, in fact, it was monotheistic as all of Job's faith, trust, and confidence was in *Elohim*. In the climactic ending of his trial, Job's faith had broadened considerably as he moved in personal relationship with *Yahweh*. His worldview also had been expanded beyond the in-the-box limits of juridical retribution to an acceptance of God's sovereign ways, which in Job's own life experience were beyond theodicy, even beyond any measure of human comprehension period.

The term *theodicy* has been a part of theological and philosophical vocabulary for approximately three hundred years, and it has motivated much debate, especially in Old Testament literature. The books of Psalms, Ecclesiastes, Jeremiah, and especially Job are sources of the material of theodicy. The German philosopher and metaphysician, Gottfried W. von Leibniz (1646-1716) was credited with coining the word *theodicy*.[25] The idea of theodicy deals with the issues of God (Gr. *theos*) and justice (Gr. *dike*). The reason that this idea becomes a problem for theologians and philosophers alike is the presence of evil in the world. To a large degree, the question of evil also affects the life of each believer as it touches all of our lives from the first case of the colic as an infant to the final heart failure. As to how theodicy relates to people, the questioning of God's justice then is twofold: (1) how is it that evil happens to obedient people? and, (2) how is it that good happens to disobedient people?

We cannot judge, either after the fact or before the fact with certainty, what God's reasons were for allowing evil to enter His universe, nor should we even try to justify Him for that act. **The *rah*, evil, which God has allowed, was and is one of the great mysteries of our omniscient sovereign Lord. His wisdom trumps all human attempts to explain.** Isaiah was right when, as a channel of the Holy Spirit, he wrote, "For as the heavens are higher than the earth, so are my ways higher than your ways, and my thoughts than your thoughts." (Isaiah 55:9) **Once again, we must by faith accept and trust Father's mysterious ways.**

As to the book of Job, the dialogue between the friends and Job is an extended confrontation about retributive justice or theodicy against Job's existential world. For Job, God's justice, seen in punishment for the wicked and prosperity (blessing) for the righteous, was not working. In fact, his experience was just the opposite. There are modern theodicists who, despite God's sanctioning of Job, still accuse him of sin so they may maintain their pat little formulas of retribution. They ignore the totality of the witness of the book by selectively dismembering the text in order to justify their claims of truth. How one approaches theodicy as it relates to the evil that caused Job's suffering in innocence depends largely on the vantage point or perspective. Whether you are a victim, or an onlooker makes all the difference in how you respond to the *rah*, evil, in life. When it is not your experience, it is easy to preach an Eliphaz kind of sermon, but when you are in a Job syndrome, all the platitudes, clichés, and "encouraging" words just do not help much. They certainly don't tell you why!

The New Testament treatment of theodicy is almost nonexistent. **What the New Testament does do is to show how God has dealt with the problem of evil.** The theologian Brueggemann stated that the New Testament made "the claim that in Jesus of Nazareth all of the unfinished business with evil is finally resolved, for in the cross and resurrection of Jesus, the power of evil and death are fully and finally overcome."[26] The victory of Christ at Calvary is so very significant to theodicy in that He was the Lamb slain from the foundation of the world. Before evil entered the universe, God had determined the plan of redemption of all creation, especially mankind. The important point here is this: **we cannot afford to get bogged down in the questions of how and why evil came to be in this world, but rather, we should glory in the cross of our Lord Jesus Christ Who laid down His life for His friends (that would be all of us)** in total submission to God's eternal plan of redeeming love for all who have been affected by the evil of this age.

The very idea of theodicy does leave serious questions

to those of a philosophical bent, but I question the need to go there. **Does God, Who is altogether God, need man, who obviously is not even god, to explain and justify His ways? Can man, who is a source of, and a contributor to evil, fathom why God permitted the evil when the Bible (even Job) does not try to explain it?** Could it possibly be that laypeople, pastors, and theologians are still yielding to the temptation to "be as gods, knowing good and evil?" (Gen. 3:5). Let every would-be theodicist repeat after Job, "[T]herefore have I uttered that I understood not; things too wonderful for me, which I knew not. . .Wherefore I abhor myself, and repent in dust and ashes" (Job 42:3b, 6).

It is time that the Church, especially the world of Christian scholars, accepts the mysteries of God. We cannot and should not be able to explain all His ways. I have a very good friend, Lynn, who is semi-retired from being a world-class magician (who also helped me do research for this writing). I have so often tried to figure out how he does those amazing effects (I call them "tricks," or more properly "illusions"). I have never asked him, "How?" I have heard other people rudely ask. Actually, the enjoyment and thrill of watching him perform is a result of not knowing how it is done. Could it be that Father knows that we can enjoy our relationship with Him far more when some of His ways remain mysterious? I should note that Lynn has also experienced the Job syndrome through very difficult reversals and transitions as well as physical suffering. Yet his faith remains stronger than ever. More than most Christians, Lynn has an appreciation for the mysterious side of God's ways.

This is a recurring question in this writing, "Why do we insist that all of God's ways must be explainable?" By now, I hope we are discovering that God is truly omniscient, and that goes far, yes, very far beyond the explainable!

Job's Syndrome

As described previously, Job's symptoms of his undesirable condition had left him in a mental and emotional state of extreme pain. One cannot suffer such loses of wealth, livelihood, reputation, and relationships without being thrown into an extreme mourning and sorrow. Job was not superhuman. His suffering was as real as ours. Since each of his loses took away a significant part of his identity, Job began questioning who he was and why he existed. People have lost businesses and some relationships before and managed to survive, but Job lost everything plus all ten children in one day. Losing things is one thing. Losing children is a loss of an entirely different nature and scale. Even these incredible loses did not cause Job to stumble in his faith. So, *the Satan* attacked his body!

The various attempts of commentators to label Job's disease as a type of leprosy, elephantiasis, or some other skin disorder are unacceptable to me. In the summer between the third and fourth grades in school, I suffered an outbreak of boils. The pain and agitation of those boils are still a very vivid memory. Over the period of three months, twenty-seven boils erupted in various places in my body, legs and arms. The life cycle of a boil was approximately two and a half to three weeks. As many as four or five boils were present at a time. The pain was similar to a bad acne pimple only multiplied by a factor of fifty (maybe a very slight exaggeration), because the infection comes from much deeper in the flesh. The pain had elements of an itch but an extremely painful itch. Job's "potsherd" (2:8) is a completely understandable tool. The relief, after an eruption of the hard core of the infection, was so remarkable that it was cause for celebration. The doctor's diagnosis was inconclusive, but he believed that the problem was from an infection. This affliction perfectly paralleled Job's condition with the notable exception that Job was covered from the crown of his head to the soles of his feet. Dr. Vij (from southern England, United Kingdom), a medical doctor, surgeon, author of several medical books, as well as two excellent books exposing the fallacies of evolution, and a friend, recently confirmed the symptoms and causes of boils, having personally treated numerous cases.[27] He agreed that such a condition could cause great pain. I can vouch for the total misery of such an affliction as the infection and fever ravaged my body continuously without any time at all for relief.

Another phase of Job's trial was the critical component, which was cosmic in its breadth and eternal in its effect. Would Job do as *the Satan* had charged God that he would do? All was on the line. In the heavenly court, God's confidence in Job waited to be vindicated. On earth, Job's destiny hung in a precarious balance. **Would Job lose his trust in *El Shaddai* and curse Him? The decision was Job's alone.**

Job's suffering was uncontrollable. Modern pain medications might have assisted had they been available. There was no help of any kind and no relief physically or emotionally. **Now spiritually, God was uncontrollable also! He was not observably active within the familiar box of promises and laws. Suddenly, God was no longer predictable!** Job knew he was innocent and living righteously. By the rules of retribution, he should be continuing in God's favor and prosperity. Maybe, like a bad dream, the calamities would be temporary, and the blessing would take over and replace the pain. But, that just did not happen! Days, weeks, and, most probably, months passed, and God was still nowhere to be found. Job as an innocent righteous man was suffering the full gamut of his "complex of symptoms." It is so very difficult to wrap one's mind around the idea of suffering at all, but especially, when it is that of the innocent and undeserving. Professor Zuck stated that, in adversity, **God might have other purposes besides retribution for wrongdoing.**[28] Job was experiencing the other purposes, what Zuck called **"the mystery of unmerited misery."**[29]

Job had friends who came from their three respective countries with very good intentions to be helpful and comfort Job in his suffering. How their friendship with Job had begun is unknown, but it must be assumed that their friendship was genuine. These friends certainly did very well at being empathetic at the beginning of their visit, but that did not last long when their pat theology seemed threatened. Dhorme translated the scene in Chapter two, verses twelve and thirteen:

> They lifted their eyes from afar and did not recognise [sic] him. Then they raised their voices and wept; they tore each one his garment and sprinkled dust on their heads. Then they sat down on the ground with him, seven days and seven nights; and no one spoke a word to him, for they saw that his suffering was very great.

These three friends soon turned their empathy into criticism of Job for not confessing his obvious sin, since they believed fully in the doctrine of divine retribution, which was the only perception they could believe at that time. From their theological mindsets, **Job's friends began to try to convince him, each in his own way that his sin had resulted in this punishment** (4:7-11; 5:8-16; 8:3, 11-22; 18:5-21). Their arguments were more than a taunt. The ideas were actually a real temptation to Job to make an admission, which would fit the doctrine of retribution, but in Job's case, it would be a lie since Job had not sinned. James E. Smith's description was concise. He explained that Eliphaz was a "mystic type" basing his argument on a vision from God. Bildad was a "traditionalist" who argued from time-honored concepts of justice. Zophar was the "dogmatist" whose position was validated by a consensus of human wisdom on the subject. Finally, Elihu, who was not one of the three friends but was the youngest of the interlocutors, stressed that God refines people through suffering; yet, he also accused Job of sin.[30]

Although Job continued to deal with his own concepts of retributive justice, his conflict with his friends was over his assertion of his innocence. It not only was conflicting with the friends; Job was agonizing with that contradiction within himself. He knew he was innocent, but he also thought he was being punished (19:1-11). The dilemma was for what reason? **Job must comprehend that his suffering was for "no reason" (at least not one which could be explained) before he could know that his love and obedience to God must also be for "no reason." That had been the challenge of** *the Satan.* **Job alone proceeded through faith and faithfulness to prove that he did serve God for "no reason," "for naught" (1:9).**

Job's comforters spoke of God beyond human reach, but still they did not doubt their own ability to articulate the pattern of His ways (theodicy). In other words, **they thought God was explainable. They missed it. God said they missed it,** "The Lord said to Eliphaz the Temanite, My wrath is kindled against thee, and against thy two friends: for ye have not spoken of me the thing that is right, as my servant Job hath." (42:7) Job's friends had spoken about God in ways He did not approve, while Job spoke to God, even challenging the relationship, yet he was approved.

Eliphaz, Bildad, and Zophar, Job's friends, spoke from an ignorant self-righteousness. These men were not mentally deficient, but in trying to explain Job's relationship to God and God's relationship to Job, they were in over their heads. They had no comprehension of the fact that God had chosen Job for the trial over them precisely because he was more righteous and faith-filled than they were. God trusted Job because He knew the heart of the man. He did not trust the friends for the very same reason. He knew their hearts also. In fact, as they talked on and on to Job, they revealed flaws in their theology, since they did not speak of God "the thing that is right..." Had the friends been given the same, or even a similar, test, they would have failed miserably. They did not understand God's gracious kindness in not allowing them the same kind of trial as Job's.

The Job syndrome is now defined: his history of wealth and position, his tragic loss of possessions, his devastating loss of ten children, his excruciating affliction, and the opposition of his wife. To be added to the list of "complex symptoms" was the mental distress and the soul shaking of the theological contradiction and criticism of his friends. The mental and emotional stresses must have been overwhelming. Job was constantly responding in desperate language. **Job, from his perspective, had been abandoned by God. He was totally on his own. He had no sense of God's guidance or presence. At that point in time, he did not know that by God's decree he would not die. He knew his theological world had been forced into a drastic change from the familiar. He knew *Elohim* was there somewhere. He could no longer explain *Elohim*'s ways in the simple** terminology of his friends. What Job did know, he only knew from his heart, **"He may slay me, I'll not quaver. I will defend my conduct to [H]is face"** (13:15, Pope).

MY PRAYER

Elohim, Lord of creation, and my God, again and again I am overwhelmed with profound emotions as I identify with your noble and faithful servant, Job. I, too, am facing my own crisis of faithfulness in suffering. Right now, with all my heart and love, I resolve to trust You unreservedly, ultimately, and completely. As You have been faithful in times past to heal, provide, protect, and preserve, I expect You to be faithful in all Your ways in my future. With a grateful heart and in biblical "hope," I await my deliverance from this present trial. Amen!

4
THE THEOLOGY OF THE BOOK OF JOB
PART ONE

> For God is not a man like me, whom I could answer
>   when we came to trial together.
> If only there were an arbiter between us
>   who would lay his hand upon us both,
>   who would remove God's rod from me
>   so that my dread of Him would not terrify me.
> Then I would speak, and not fear Him,
>   for He is far from just to me!
>
> -Job 9:32-35 (Gordis)[31]

Dale, the oldest son of my first cousin, Lucile, experienced a Job syndrome of extreme proportions. Here is his recollection:[32]

January 20, 2000, Thursday night, ten o'clock, I was standing in my daughter's bedroom. She had a computer, and I was standing behind her as she typed out a wedding ceremony that I was to perform on Saturday...The doorbell rang...In this rural area, it was unheard of to have visitors that time of night. My heart started pounding. Being Daddy, I said, "I got it." I opened the door and standing on my porch was the pastor I had served under, and Waymon, life-long friends of mine. Neither one of them could make eye contact with me. I knew it was something serious…Waymon was trembling. Pastor had tears in his eyes. I said, "What's wrong…somebody, tell me what's wrong!" By now, I'm starting to panic…Pastor reached out his trembling hand, handing me a little slip of paper and said, "Call this number." I turned around, and they stepped on in the house. I went to the kitchen and picked up the phone to dial Sheriff Bill whom I had known my whole life. My hand was shaking so badly I was missing the numbers. I finally dialed through, and Bill answered, "Dale, I'm standing in your parent's yard…they won't let me go in…I don't know how to tell you, Buddy…your parents have been murdered."

My whole world came apart. My whole family erupted. My son, a high school track star in the eleventh grade, tore through the door and was running down the road. I gave chase for about a block, but I couldn't catch him. I walked back to the house. My wife was wailing. My girls were in the floor wailing. I haven't cried yet, because…I'm trying…to be Daddy and hold them all together…But, my heart was broken into a million pieces! Those nightmares had begun…

That is just the beginning of the story of Dale's pain on pain. The kind of pain that hurts so deep you want to die—pain that tears up physical systems, so you don't function normally. This pain destroys with emotions so intense and excessive that there is just no verbal description, which actually corresponds to the reality. It is a pain so "evil" that only God can ease or comfort or change!

Dale and I grew up in very similar backgrounds. His mother, my cousin Lucile, was closer to my dad's age. When she and her husband, Lindsey, decided to go to Bible school to prepare for ministry, my dad and our family went to the same college for the same purpose. In fact, they did ministry together on many occasions during that time. Dad and Lindsey received assistance under the GI Bill after their participation in WWII.

Growing up in a pastor's home had many joys, but it also had some unusual pressures. Dale recalled, "I was reared into an amazing Christian family for which I am always grateful…even though I was reared in a family rich in Christianity, rich in faith, and rich in ministry, I struggled as a child with fear." Dale's fears were many. He even lay in bed many nights crying from anxiety of worrying about such things as "missing the Rapture…one of my parents dying, or their getting a divorce." The fears were like horrible nightmares!

Dale's dad was an excellent preacher, teacher, and pastor, so his theological background was strong. "I heard a positive Gospel," he said. He learned the teachings of the Bible from some of the best of teachers. He continued, "I got saved at nine years old…I could take you to the exact spot…I had been to the altar many times before, but that night I got gloriously saved." Then at thirteen, at Youth Camp, he experienced the Baptism in the Holy Spirit. Even then, not all the fears were gone. There was constant worrying about loss and tragedy, but none of those things ever happened from childhood on through the teenage years.

At sixteen, Dale was called by the Holy Spirit to ministry, and he began to preach in his Dad's church and, also, some surrounding churches. After graduation, he went to a denominational college and began preparing himself for advancing the ministry. With a fire for evangelism burning in his soul, after two years of Bible college, Dale left school and began evangelizing. He met a young lady in the church where his dad pastored at that time, and they soon got married. Their lives together were started in ministry. All was well and progressed through evangelizing, serving as a minister of music, and pastoring for several years.

Dale and his wife had no children. Dale said, "I had accepted the fact…that is where the fear came back in…I was afraid of having children…I didn't want to bring them into this world…afraid of this, afraid of that." He was somewhat relieved with their circumstance, but after some time, a miracle (the doctor said it was a miracle) happened, and they had a daughter. She quickly became the apple of Dale's eye. "She had me around her little finger from day one," was his comment. From that new beginning, they began to enjoy their new role as parents.

Dale felt that one child was enough, but still they continued to try for a pregnancy. Surprisingly, they suddenly were expecting another child. Their son was born with difficulties. The baby was born prematurely and had to be incubated for a period of time. He was born into an emotionally stressed situation.

Yet, beyond Dale's emotional storms, the denomination promoted Dale to the position of State Youth Director in another state. This went well, but problems at home were hidden in the flurry of ministry activity. Special meetings were the highlight, since he enjoyed being the "darling" in that elevated position. But, at home, it was another world. Stress almost beyond endurance was taking its toll on Dale. It was during a particularly painful episode that for the first time "divorce" was mentioned.

After his term as Director, Dale resumed a pastoral ministry back in his home state. The relationship continued to be strained. The word *divorce* continued to be used. He contemplated the children, the ministry, and his belief that God does not approve of divorce. He was torn between his belief about divorce and his need for a divorce. Dale was quick to point out that he shoulders so much of the blame. He had his share of flaws. He knew he wasn't as good a husband as he should have been. This situation worsened for several more years. As Dale poured his heart out to his dad and mom one day, his dad said, "I'm either going to have to bury you or put you in an insane asylum…" It was shortly after that when the divorce became a reality. Here is Dale's account:

> It was one of the two worst days of my life. I was sick…so sick! I went before the Judge…I lost

everything. I lost custody of my children…He made me cash in 20 years of denominational retirement and give it up…I was devastated. I lost my ministry as well. Sometime later, I drove to another city with my ordination papers in my trembling hand, and I walked up to the front door of my longtime friend and Bishop. I surrendered my papers to Pastor Woodrow, the denominational official. He was broken by this and weeping with great emotion, and he tried to comfort me and encourage me.

Dale's life was seriously affected by these events for a long time. After a period of mourning these losses, Dale was eventually happily married again and started working for himself, but it was still a while before there would be a restoration of ministry. All this time, the Holy Spirit was gently leading his life through healing of emotions and reevaluating his purpose. Dale's Job syndrome had begun, but the full force of the storm was yet to come very quickly.

There were other adversities, which brought a lot of hurt. One was a phone call (one of only two from denominational pastor friends) from a close friend of many years who "blasted me," as Dale put it. He called Dale an "idiot," a "fool," and other choice terms, because he couldn't keep his marriage together.

Dale discussed how devastated he was after the divorce, "I was angry at God; I was angry at the church…I thought no one would go to bat for me, after I had dedicated my whole life to the denomination and to

God...It seemed they just let me fall through the cracks with no second thoughts." Once again, the Job syndrome produced anger at God, because deep down we all know that the omnipotent, omniscient God must be ultimately responsible for there being no healing, resolution and peace. Dale was wrestling with all the syndrome questions we are discussing here in this book.

As Dale kept fighting through all those emotions, his shield of faith had become dented by the bombardments, but the blast of *the Satan's* strategic missile of destruction was yet to come. Although his faith was certainly assaulted, he still believed God was there and in control, but he couldn't find Him. There was a Job-like absence of His presence.

Several transitions took place with varying degrees of adversity. Dale finally settled down to living in a rural community with his new family, and eventually he had his son and daughter back home with him. He worked with dairy farmers in his business of trimming and medicating the feet of the cows, which is a necessary part of dairy farming. It was then the bomb dropped which opened this testimony. I want to pick up the story of Dale's Job syndrome from the announcement of his parents' horrendous murder.

When Dale said that all the nightmares had begun, he went on to say, "All that fear of all my life culminated right there—it all came together...the next few days were a nightmare." Dale would learn the shocking details of the murder of his precious and godly parents, and the pain would only go deeper and deeper.

The full story did not come out until the trials of the perpetrators, but here is the story in brief, as Dale pieced it together from the trial, public records of the investigation and videotaped testimonies. Two young men eighteen years old, who had helped Lindsey in the hay fields the summer before, knocked on his door wanting to use the phone. They had cheated a drug dealer out of a $20 cocaine rock by slipping him $1 instead. Naturally, the dealer chased them. They had fled by car in the direction of Lindsey's farm, but going the back way they came upon a barrier, abandoned the vehicle, and continued to flee on foot into the wooded area at the back of the farm. The chasers came up on the abandoned car and proceeded to destroy it with baseball bats by beating it, breaking windows, and flattening the tires. When the young men thought it was safe, they smoked that one rock and walked across the pasture to Lindsey and Lucile's house about 7:30 that night with the intention of stealing their car.

Lindsey and Lucile were sitting in their matching recliner chairs eating popcorn. Lindsey answered the door, and within thirty minutes, they were both dead. The guys had taken the butcher knives from the kitchen and stabbed Lucile 34 times. Dale recalled with great emotion, "Dad had been stabbed 23 times and his throat had been cut…he had been beaten until you couldn't recognize him—his head was nearly twice its normal size…he had been kicked in the groin many, many times…apparently he was trying to crawl to get to a gun." Dale continued barely holding back the flood of pain, "Well…the horror!…Not just losing your parents at the same time, but the manner of their death."

Lindsey was 71 years old, and Lucile was 67. They were healthy and happy. Then, in 30 minutes of evil, they were dead from "horror movie" assaults. Instantly, things changed in Dale's life. He said, "I just didn't understand…I was the oldest of two brothers…the mantle fell on me, and it fell on me heavily…It hit me like a ton of bricks that suddenly I was the oldest member of the family, and that I had the responsibility of making some hard decisions." Some of those decisions were concerning the memorial arrangements.

My two brothers, Troy and Lemuel, and I participated in the memorial service with music. We even tried to be of some help, as did many others, but really, Dale was walking his journey of grief alone. Dale put it this way, "A heavy weight fell on me, not just my grief, not just my sorrow, not just my confusion, not just my fear, but the weight of my family fell on me, too."

Although there were moments of reprieve when the load was eased a little, Dale continued in deep grief for about four weeks. After the funeral and a few days of tying up loose ends, Dale went back home to try to work. Being self-employed, he needed to work. As a "bovine hoof trimmer," the jobs were physically taxing, so at first, he only worked about a half of a day at a time. His employers at the different farms were understanding, patient, and accommodating because of the circumstances.

On a particular day, Dale was set up in the middle of a large pasture, isolated, even using a generator for electricity. He had a contraption that was a kind of chute. It was also a tilt table. He would drive the cow into it, strap her in, and tilt the cow on its side to take care of its feet. His primary tool for this was a pair of nips a little over a foot long, which had to be replaced about every other month, and they cost about $100 each. So, they were a valuable tool. Here is Dale's account of that day:

> I was trying, but my heart wasn't in it. My mind was just on Mama and Daddy and my loss. I was trying to pray, and I couldn't pray…I could not pray! I had not been able to really pray like I wanted to since their deaths. Finally, in frustration, it had come to a head. I let a cow down and turned her out…Suddenly, it just came over me. With my nippers in my hand, I started running across the pasture. I ran until I was exhausted, and I was crying every step of the way…not just crying. I was wailing. All of what was in me was coming out…all the bitterness in my soul. When I couldn't run any farther, I stopped, and I threw those nippers at God as hard as I could. I gave it everything I had, and I threw them as high as I could. I slung them into the heavens, and shook my fist at God and said, "I am so angry, and I am so hurt! I don't understand why you let this happen!"
>
> When I said that, I fell in a heap on the ground. It was like every bit of strength came out of me, and I could not stand. I didn't lie down, and I didn't sit down. I fell down. I fell as if I were dead…and, that

day I did do some dying. When I fell, finally after four weeks, I felt Him put His arms around me...I felt His love, and I felt His comfort. He just wrapped me in His arms, and I lay on the ground and softly wept...He loved me, and He comforted me. I don't know how long I was there, but when I got up, I was transformed! Did I still hurt—yes! Did I still grieve—yes! Did I have answers—no! But, I had Him!

From that day on, Dale was in a process of healing. At first, every day was a bad day. He cried and grieved every day. Then only three or four days a week were so full of grief. Little by little, his heavy grieving left. Now after many, many years, only one or two days a year are spent in "missing them so much." Dale made the observation that the often-used phrase "time heals" is a lie. He said, "God may use time, but He is the Healer."

There is a part of the story of Lucile's murder that I must add to this collection on the Job syndrome. Going through the legal events that led to the conviction of both young men, Dale had to sit through the video of the questioning of the one who killed his mother. The officer asked him why they were there. He said, "Our car wouldn't run; we were there to steal the...car." They did steal the car after the murders. Then the officer asked, "Why didn't you just take the car and leave?" He said, "Well, when I demanded the car, the woman...reached in her purse sittin' on the bar, got out the keys and tossed 'em to me...I caught 'em and put 'em in my pocket." The investigator said, "You had what you wanted—why didn't you just leave?" The answer was, "I don't know. I just couldn't leave yet…Something just came over me…" The officer said, "I can understand you were afraid that he (Lindsey) might get a gun if you let him live, but what about her? Why did you kill the lady?" That's when he said, "She looked at me, and pointed her finger at me, and started speaking at me in a foreign language…when she did, something inside of my head said, 'you gotta shut her up…shut her up…you've got to stop her'…so, I killed her."

Lucile had never learned another language other than English. She, being full of the Holy Spirit, had often prayed "with the Spirit" (1 Corinthians 14:14-15). I will not try to explain this phenomenon here, but this is my summation of what happened. The demon(s) in that young man reacted to the Holy Spirit in Lucile, and the evil spirit of murder manifested. I think Dale assessed it beautifully when he said, "Mama left this world speaking in tongues!"

This testimony of Dale's Job syndrome has touched on all the elements of a Job-type life experience. Dale has gone on to pastor a church for nine years. He then accepted a position to teach music in a high school. He added to that a position of Minister of Music in a prominent church in his community for several years. He is now successfully pastoring again. **He still does not have answers to the big questions, but his message is, "Trust God!"—a message of VICTORY!** Once again, a true Job syndrome leads one into a new life and a new relationship with God.

Trust produces peace! Whether circumstances change immediately or not, trust Him.

Dale recalled that another one of our cousins spoke to him at the funeral of Lindsey and Lucile. She greeted him with tears running down her cheeks; then spoke these life-changing and profound words, "This has forced me to rethink my **theology** (emphasis mine). I never believed God would allow something like this to happen to saintly people of great faith."

Introductory Thoughts on the Theology of Job

The word "theology" far too often among Christians is viewed with a negative connotation. In fact, in some circles, this word is disdained for its association with scholars and critical interpretation of Scripture. Actually, theology is a very good word which means having a body of knowledge of God (Greek *theos* meaning *God*, and from the root *logos* which means *communication, reasoning, logic, computation, or collection of thoughts, words or sayings*). I think all Christians are theologians, since they should know God experientially and know about God as a basis for faith. Two verses markedly illustrate the point.

> But without faith it is impossible to please him: for he that cometh to God must believe that he is, and that he is a rewarder of them that diligently seek him.
> -Hebrews 11:6

> Till we all come in the unity of the faith, and of the knowledge of the Son of God, unto a perfect man,

unto the measure of the stature of the fulness of Christ.

-Ephesians 4:13

The quoted passage beginning this chapter is an example in Job, which is loaded with concepts exhibiting superior theology. Job stated, "God is not a man." That is weighty! Job clearly understood that God is "other" than man. He does not walk, talk, think, or act like men. All of God's ways are vastly above and beyond the ways of men, and not just quantitatively. They are qualitatively whole, right, just, divine—PERFECT. Words like *excel* and *supersede* do not apply to God. Unlike man, He cannot be quantified! All words of comparison fail miserably, since in all of His traits and characteristics, He is beyond comparison. At this point, I must quote a part of a yet to be published book by my son, Gabriel (Dr. Miller). He was the sick infant whose story is told in Chapter 1. From the book, *Ultimate Reality*, hear what he says about God being incomparable:

> …a case has been laid out for two types or levels of reality. The conclusion can be summarized fairly concisely: A Creator must be more real, must exist more fully, must be more alive than His creation. And although this is basically the point I wish to make, my choice of words has nearly shot my arguments in the foot. For when we take a step back and think about it, *more* doesn't have anything to do with it. *More* is a comparative. *More* puts Creator and creation on the same scale. *More* is an impossibility.

Equally impossible is *most*, or any other superlative, for superlatives also represent a place on the scale. Whatever attributes one would posit the Creator to have, whether greatness or goodness or something else similar, we must not put Him on the same scale as us. A Creator could not possibly be the greatest or the best. If He is great and good, then He must be the essence and source of greatness and goodness. He would not be great or good in the sense of exhibiting a degree of greatness or goodness; rather He would be all that it means to be great and good. This is something altogether different. This is what it means for there to be an absolute. A Creator cannot be the greatest or the best because that would put Him on the scales of greatness and goodness. The Creator cannot be on the scale; the Creator is the scale. A Creator is by His very essence the absolute standard for everything. Creator-reality, therefore, is absolute reality.[33]

Gabriel has said it so well. All our words of comparison fail when trying to describe God. Yet, even the Bible uses comparative words in speaking of Him. The words of Job, "God is not a man like me," make us realize that he understood more than most the otherness of God.

Job, in our introductory passage, also mentioned an "arbiter" who could lay his hand on man and God at the same time. Here, again, is both a powerful and noble theological concept, which foreshadows doctrines of the New Testament, which are revealed and explained in the person of Jesus. Job's question anticipates the coming of Christ Who is the God-man. The One whom the Bible calls a "mediator."

> For there is one God, and one mediator between God and men, the man Christ Jesus.
> -1 Timothy 2:5

What Job is questioning, as a possibility, has in the person of Jesus, become a reality. Jesus is the One Who makes it possible to be constantly connected to and related to God.

As we begin to open our minds to the theological concepts, which are to be treated in this chapter and the following chapter, we will be developing the basis for faith. It is only a foundational knowledge of God that will support true faith to strengthen one in the storm of trial and to weather the battering of evil, which rolls in wave after wave after wave.

The Validity of the Book of Job

The book of Job has witnesses to its validity in both the Old and the New Testaments. This is a necessary point. Despite the naysayers and liberal critics of the Scripture, these biblical witnesses to Job clearly establish the book as a part of the Holy Bible. Traditionally, interpreters within the church have emphasized the long-suffering and patient Job of the prologue based on the reference of the apostle James, "Behold, we count them happy which endure. Ye have heard of the patience of Job, and have seen the end of the Lord; that the Lord is very pitiful, and of tender mercy"

(James 5:11). Although there have been attempts to discredit this interpretation by James, this reference of James is extremely important at two levels. First, James is validating the life of Job and the book, which tells Job's story. Second, James is encouraging his fellow Jewish Christians to endure patiently their persecutions with an illustration in Job with which they are very familiar. There are other references in the New Testament which seem to be quoted from Job such as Peter's statement that our trial of faith is as gold tried in the fire (1 Peter 1:7 compared to Job 23:10). Such references do give weight to the argument of the validity of the book of Job.

The Old Testament witness to the book of Job is in the writing of Ezekiel, "Though Noah, Daniel, and Job were in it, as I live, saith the LORD God, they shall deliver neither son nor daughter; they shall but deliver their own souls by their righteousness" (Ezek. 14:20). In this prophetic passage, the "Lord" named these three men twice (14:14, 20) and prophesied four times (14:14, 16, 18, 20) that not even the righteousness of these great men would save the nation of Israel from the judgment, which was coming.

There are several Old Testament books, which have verses similar to verses in Job. Many of these references are from Jeremiah, the Psalms, Proverbs, Isaiah, Zechariah and Malachi.[34] Although many scholars, who date the book of Job late, believe Job is quoting the other writers, there are good reasons to espouse the priority of Job.

The book of Job is well attested in the Scripture and firmly entrenched in the canon, the Holy Bible. It was accepted very early in both the rabbinic traditions and, also, among the early Christian fathers. The questioning of the validity of Job has actually been a very late development by those liberal writers who also question much of the Bible. For those of us who hold tenaciously to the doctrine of verbal inspiration, there can be no doubt then that whatever the book of Job offers pertaining to theology may be received in full confidence as the Word of God—part of the Holy Bible.

The Worship of One God in Job

I feel we should take some time to contemplate Job's profound monotheism as contrasted to the polytheism of the society in which he lived. Job's world bore remarkable similarities to our society as so many make gods of people and things other than God our Lord. The clans, tribes, and nations surrounding Job's immediate world were engrossed in polytheistic beliefs. An illustration is found in chapter nine where four constellations are named: Arcturus (Bear), Orion, Pleiades, and "the Chambers of the South." Job referred to these constellations as a matter of fact, as he spoke of God's ability to create and maintain the universe. Although Job recognized their existence, he did not believe their idolatrous associations nor practice the related cultic rites. John E. Hartley gave a brief summary of the meanings of these constellations:

> The stars, by reason of their brilliance and their movement, attracted the wonder and worship of the

ancient Semites, above all the Mesopotamians. Believed to be gods and goddesses, the heavenly bodies had a prominent role in the pantheon, e.g., Anu (heavens), Shamash (sun), Sin (moon), and Ishtar (Venus). Those who worshipped the stars absorbed themselves in studying their movements in order to divine their messages and gain insight into the future.[35]

Although this idolatrous polytheism was prevalent in Job's world, it did not affect his belief in one God. Job worshipped one God, talked to one God, described one God, and finally responded to the one God of the Whirlwind.

In the book of Job, the use of several of the Old Testament names of God does not in any way indicate a polytheistic tendency. The skilled use of the synonymous, or nearly synonymous, names by the speakers in the book and the author show their understanding of the subtle shadings of difference in usage of the names. In some examples, the choices may have been arbitrary, or the chosen name fit the poetry better. In most other instances of use, the name chosen has a discernable repetition of use with the subject at hand. **The name that most often appears in Job is *Elohim* or its other form *Eloah*.** This name is translated "God" in the Authorized Version and means the one and only Creator God. **The name *Shaddai* or *El Shaddai* is most often translated "the Almighty" and designates God Who is omnipotent or all-powerful.** It is profound that the title *Shaddai* is used thirty-one times by the Job writer yet only occurs sixteen times in the rest of the Old Testament. **It seems that the Holy Spirit, in the Job writer, would have us understand that, no matter what is going on in our lives, God is still the Almighty. The use of the name *Yahweh*, or the Hebrew tetragrammaton *YHWH*, has a definite significance in each usage in Job.** The use of *Yahweh* is easily recognized in the King James Version as well as most other translations in English by its spelling "LORD." (In this writing, I follow the convention of spelling this name "Lord" except in direct quotes from scripture.) It is used as God's personal name as distinct from other names used in reference to God as a concept or a force. Where God appears or speaks in person, He is *Yahweh*. Where His power, His actions, His thoughts, His demands, or His doctrines are in view, one of His other names is employed.

Yahweh is the name spoken to Moses in Exodus 6:2-3, "And God spoke unto Moses, and said unto him, I am the LORD: And I appeared unto Abraham, unto Isaac, and unto Jacob by the name of God Almighty (*El Shaddai*), but by my name JEHOVAH (*Yahweh*) was I not known to them..." (Parenthesis are mine). Wolfers gave an excellent treatment on the use of the names of God. On the use of *Yahweh*, the Lord, he wrote, "We are thus certainly encountering in the Book [sic] of Job a convention in the use of the Divine names which is unique to that Book, with a very meticulous restriction placed on the use of 'The Lord' as an indication of His 'presence' and personality as distinct from His function, status or power."[36]

At times in Job, these three names of God seem to have an interplay, which augments the meaning of the passage. One such instance is seen in Job 40:1-2, "Moreover the LORD answered Job, and said, Shall he that contendeth with the Almighty instruct him? he that reproveth God, let him answer it." Here *Yahweh*, the present One, is pointing out that Job has been contending with *Shaddai*, the all-powerful One, and questioning or reproving *Elohim*, his own Creator. Clearly, this verse is not suggesting three gods, but one God in three aspects or characteristics.

We should conclude then that **Job himself is the servant of one God. He is not confused. He "fears" the Creator, the one Lord of the universe. He is monotheistic through and through. As a matter of fact, his three friends and Elihu are all monotheistic. They too serve and follow the one true Almighty God. This was for Job, and is for us, the foundational basis for all faith. None will spiritually survive a Job syndrome without absolute trust in the one revealed God of the Bible.**

The Attributes of God in the Book of Job

Throughout the book of Job there are allusions to the sovereignty of God. In 12:13-25, for example, Job recounted the actions of the sovereign God. Among the actions listed there are the following, according to Hartley's translation: "He destroys," "He imprisons," "He holds back," "He releases," "He controls," "He leads counselors" and "priests," "He makes nations great, then destroys them," "He deprives the leaders" and "He makes them wander."[37] From the beginning of the book, Job sees God as sovereign in being and in action. Fyall asked the question concerning Job at the end of his trial, "What is it that Job now knows? First, he is convinced of God's sovereignty over the universe."[38] Job had said, "I know that [Y]ou can do all things. No purpose of [Y]ours can be foiled," (42:2, translated by Hartley).[39] It is fascinating to me that the word *purpose* here is from the Hebrew *mezimma*, the same word used in Jeremiah 23:20 translated "thoughts." "The anger of the LORD will not turn back until He has executed and performed the thoughts of His heart. In the latter days you will understand it perfectly." (NKJV) The word means the will or purpose of God in these verses. It is clear that Job has come to submit completely to his sovereign Lord. He has yielded to His "purpose." **This is an extremely important part of Job's process through his syndrome. Job yielded to the mysterious will and purpose of God.** Even though he was soon to be at the end of his trial and still did not comprehend a reason. In his God encounter, he submitted to God's higher "purpose."

The first part of verse 42:2 shows that Job had confirmed his faith in *El Shaddai*, the Almighty, for he said, "[Y]ou can do all things." Early in the dialogue (6:14), Job had respect for the Almighty. Toward the end of his trial, in his last speeches (31:2, 35) he was respecting God's omnipotence calling Him by the name *Shaddai*. All through the dialogue, each of the interlocutors had praised the works of God's power and often had used the name *Shaddai*. This attribute of God, which is omnipotence, is well attested in the book of Job, although Job himself in his anger and frustration seemed to express ambivalence as he questioned whether God might have limitations. What is clear is that in chapter forty-two, all of Job's questions have been resolved, and for him God is all-powerful. **An acceptance of and resignation to God's omnipotence is absolutely necessary for faith to be sustained through a Job syndrome.**

The attribute of God most called into question by the book of Job is the justice of God. The questioning revolves around the doctrine of retribution. To be more precise, it is "the doctrine of individual retribution, or terrestrial eschatology, as it has been called, the doctrine that righteousness always brings prosperity and wickedness misfortune, in this life," as Pope has discussed.[40] Sarcastically, Pope continued, "The dogma is doubtless a great comfort to the healthy and prosperous, but a cruel taunt to the sick and poor."[41] Wow! What an insightful observation! Pope's sarcasm does grasp the essence of one of the most painful aspects of ministry to those in suffering.

This very problem is one of my pet peeves and is one of the major reasons I write this book. **When we use the tried and tired clichés of the doctrine of retribution in our feeble attempts to comfort the hurting, we surely "taunt" them in a cruel manner. Even when we use**

misapplied Scripture, it often exacerbates the Job syndrome in which these precious faithful ones are suffering. As with Job's comforters, our words can quickly be the source of additional pain, discouragement, irritation, frustration, and self-doubt. Again and again in my ministry, I have seen the pain of self-deprecation because one did not seem to have the same faith as a friend who constantly talked of "positive confession" and bragged concerning their health and prosperity. As Job's suffering was intensified by his comparison with his friends' seemingly more righteous and faith-filled examples, so often those in the Job syndrome suffer even more with similar comparisons by their "friends." In the example of Dale and his parents above, he was devastated with a similar comparison when certain "friends" accused Lindsey and Lucille of having sin in their lives, or they would not have suffered such a death. How horrible to add to the pain of the family with such an uncaring and asinine accusation!

As one goes through a Job syndrome, many questions erupt out of these kinds of comparison. "I know I live better than he does; why am I suffering while he seems to be so blessed?" "I have tried to speak only those things which should bring peace, health and material plenty; why doesn't it work for me?" "I have reminded God and quoted His promises over and over; why isn't He listening?" "It has been years since I started suffering with these problems; why am I still not healed or delivered?"

In Job's case, one of the major aspects of these

comparisons had to do with the idea of retribution. The reward or punishment of the doctrine of retribution is often expounded concerning Israel and its neighboring nations in the Old Testament (Lev. 26; Deut. 28; Jer. 12; 14; 17). The blessings or punishments are also pronounced on the obedient or disobedient individuals (Ps. 1; 37; Isa. 68:6-14; Ezek. 18). Pope explained that this view is "orthodox," since its implication is "normative for the Old Testament."[42] **There should be no exceptions to such a precise and fair doctrine, and this was exactly the point for the argument of Job's friends. Yet, in the Old Testament, the very opposite seems to be the case on occasion.** The writer of Ecclesiastes observed, "There is a vanity which is done upon the earth; that there be just men, unto whom it happeneth according to the work of the wicked; again, there be wicked men, to whom it happeneth according to the work of the righteous..." (Eccl. 8:14). The translators of the New International Version captured the precise meaning of this verse with this, "There is something else meaningless that occurs on earth: righteous men who get what the wicked deserve, and wicked men who get what the righteous deserve. This too, I say, is meaningless." **By inspiration of the Holy Spirit, Solomon is telling us that the doctrine of retribution is not always applicable in the here and now of our everyday lives.**

Abel offered a sacrifice pleasing to God, but his brother Cain violently murdered him. Joseph had revelatory dreams from God but was sold into slavery where he spent several years in misery before he was blessed with a turn around. David was anointed king of Israel, yet for years he lived in exile fleeing for his very life before he came into the kingdom. Uriah was a devout man faithful to God, his wife, and his king, but his wife was stolen, and he was murdered on a battlefield. Naboth was faithful to God in guarding his family inheritance by refusing to sell his vineyard to King Ahab, but he was falsely accused and died a horrible death by stoning. Jeremiah moved under a heavy anointing as a mighty prophet of God, but he was beaten and imprisoned on several occasions and threatened with death more than once. The book to the Hebrews described many of the Old Testament heroes in 11:36-38,

> And others had trial of cruel mockings and scourgings, yea, moreover of bonds and imprisonment: They were stoned, they were sawn asunder, were tempted, were slain with the sword: they wandered about in sheepskins and goatskins; being destitute, afflicted, tormented; (Of whom the world was not worthy:) they wandered in deserts, and in mountains, and in dens and caves of the earth.

We can add Job to this list of great and righteous men to whom gross evil came testing their faith to the breaking point. **These are just a few of a number of biblical characters who suffered from unmerited evil. Once again, we see contradictions to the always in force, here and now, law of retribution. "Here and now" is a key phrase to understanding my argument. The fact of** ultimate retribution in the eternal hereafter is never a question. The righteous will ultimately be rewarded, and the wicked will ultimately be punished. But, the deserved reward or punishment in the "here and now" is postponed during a Job syndrome, once again, testing the faith of the sufferer to the extreme as "gold...tried with fire." (1 Peter 1:7)

In chapter twenty-one, Job put forth a major argument against the doctrine of retribution. He asked questions impossible to answer and listed a series of benefits the wicked have in disregard to their wickedness. Job explained that the wicked grow old and become mighty; their children are well established; their homes are safe; God does not use His rod on them; their livestock flourish; they have many children; they sing and dance; they live in prosperity; and, they die quickly (implying without much suffering) (21:7-13). The wicked enjoy all of these benefits while they rebel against and reject God (21:14-15). In his argument, Job proceeded with tough sarcastic questions in verses 17 and 18:

> How often is the lamp of the wicked snuffed out,
>   or does calamity come on them,
>   or pains which God apportions in [H]is anger?
> How often do they become like straw before the
>   wind and
>   like chaff that the storm snatches away?
> (Hartley)[43]

Hartley remarked, "Each of Job's questions expect the answer 'very few times, if any.' But any exception to the application of the law of retribution means that it cannot be applied categorically."⁴⁴ **The argument of Job's friends was that retribution is always in effect in the present. Seeing that their position was not the strongest, in order to have a back door to their contention, Eliphaz (in 5:4) and Zophar (in 20:1) introduced the idea of delayed retribution.** This meant that punishment for wrongdoing would not be exacted in the life of the perpetrator but would be the inherited experience in the lives of that person's offspring. Job strongly denied the validity of their reasoning (21:19-21). His strong words about the evildoer were, "Let his own eyes see his ruin, / let him drink of the wrath of *Shaddai*." (21:20, Hartley).⁴⁵ In other words, Job is saying that the wicked person will ultimately suffer for his own sin, but not necessarily in this life.

Throughout the dialogue section of the book that bears his name, **Job wrestled emotionally and spiritually against the concept of divine retribution as taught by his comforters as well as within his own theological framework. His actual living experience was contradicting the misapplied theology.** This conflict called into question the absolute justice of God. About God, Dhorme stated, "His principle attribute is justice."⁴⁶ **It is the questioning of Who God really is and whether He is just that can lead into philosophical meanderings of false logic that historically have**

produced agnostics and atheists. Many intellectuals over the past two hundred plus years have rejected the God of the Bible on the basis that He is not just. Anderson summarized the process:

> The argument has been expressed with philosophical clarity as follows: If God were perfectly good, He could not tolerate the existence of violence, disease, etc.; therefore there must be some limit to His ability to control such events, that is, He is not almighty. Alternatively, if God does have complete power over everything that happens, His failure to curb the wrongs that occur must be due to the fact that He does not see anything wrong in them, that is, He is not good.[47]

The fallacy of the logic is not in the process so much as it is in the false assumptions. The critical philosopher needs to consider his very freedom to think those propositions. Alexander had the freedom to plan the conquering of most of the known world. Hitler had the freedom to devise his plan for enslaving Europe and obliterating the Jewish people. Mother Theresa had the freedom to follow Christ in ministering to the lepers, orphans, and AIDS victims in India. God could have created every person with a total inability to think wrong thoughts about Him or other persons. He could have created a perfect world free of evil, pain, or poverty (He did, as a matter of fact, the other world—heaven), but His holiness necessitated an unforced respect, love, and worship on the part of His human creatures. **All mankind in Adam sinned and came under the destructive or "fallen" influence of the Devil, therefore, sin and evil entered the world through the choices of all people in Adam.** Subsequently, the philosophical argument above is false because it assumes that a good and just God could not for any reason allow men to be evil or do evil; nor could He allow a world to exist under a curse with all its calamities. To believe in the truth of the Bible is to believe in a just God and to believe that in His justice He allows men the freedom to be right or wrong by God's own standard.

The doctrine of retribution in the book of Job is directly dependent on God's justice. **The problem for Job, as well as all who experience the Job syndrome, is a too limited view of God's justice.** Many commentators seem to see justice as synonymous with fairness. **God does not function in a one-size-fits-all fairness.** He judges each individual by His higher standard, which is also modified by mercy and grace. God's action in Eliphaz's life was not an appropriate action in Job's life. **Absolute divine retribution would be a devastating action on God's part.** The Flood, Sodom, and Gomorrah are illustrations of that kind of retribution. Nobody would even want retribution to be true all the time! Mercy is the real need, for "all have sinned, and come short of the glory of God" (Rom. 3:23). **No one would survive an absolute retribution, which was not modified by God's mercy and grace!**

It is admitted that double retribution (punishment or reward) is taught in scripture and that in many, even most, life experiences it works as taught. But, what of the Job syndrome? **Is God bound by the doctrine of retribution? Most certainly, He is not! If He had been bound by retribution as a law, He could not have allowed Job's trial in the first place. He would have broken His own law, because Job was indeed righteous by God's own admission** "...that there is none like him in the earth, a perfect and an upright man, one that feareth God, and escheweth evil" (Job 2:3). By a strict interpretation of the doctrine of retribution then as in Deuteronomy 28, God would be bound to continue to bless and prosper Job. Yet, Job suffered horrific evil, which brought him to the brink of utter destruction.

Evil or Suffering in Job

The manifestation of evil in the book of Job is the tragic sequence of events that so shockingly affected the righteous believer, the man Job. As Anderson observed, "In the story of Job, the problem of evil in the world is not dealt with abstractly, but in terms of one man's agony."[48] Human misery, or even the abstract principle of evil, is a problem for those who believe in a personal, all-powerful, and loving God. Outside of Christian faith, the explanations for evil, such as denial, limitation of God, denial of God's sovereignty and goodness, or even the denial of God's existence at all, are wholly unsatisfactory for a believer.

Especially, since the development of the so-called scientific method, men have sought to explain suffering in terms of cause and effect. Anderson again stated that men look backward connecting past sin and present suffering, which may have some legitimacy at times. Contrastingly, the Bible looks forward in hope, not in origins and causes, but in goals. Anderson understood it clearly when he wrote, **"The purpose of suffering is seen, not in its cause, but in its results."**[49] Joseph's famous statement to his brothers, even after his many years of reversals and suffering, is appropriate here, "But Joseph said to them, 'Do not be afraid, for am I in God's place? And as for you, you meant evil against me, but God meant it for good in order to bring about this present result, to preserve many people alive'" (Gen. 50:19-20, NASB).

In dealing with personal suffering, perhaps **we should discern the goals** by asking, "What will become of this?" Or, "What will this accomplish?" **If in the present sufferings, because of evil, one cannot see a goal, there should not be a denial that there is a divine goal in the making.** Then is when faith must reach out to *Yahweh*, the ever-present One, **to believe His goal is being brought to realty.**

Here is a question that should be asked. If things are set right later, after all the evil, which caused suffering, does it, or should one expect it to, neutralize all the damage done? Anderson made an astounding comment, "The biblical answer is that God (but only God!) actually transforms evil into good, so that in retrospect (but only in retrospect!) it is seen to have actually been good, without diminishing in the least the awful actuality of the evil it was at the time."[50] This is a profound statement! **God takes the evil, which *the Satan* brings into our lives and transforms it into good. He does not whitewash it. He does not redress it with a façade. But, He re-creates the evil into good!**

Many of those whom I have interviewed about their Job syndromes, who still are painfully aware of evil's devastating effects, admit that now they see the good which God meant and has created into their lives. Remember in Ron and Vicki's story, Vicki said, "There's a feeling that I went through. I don't understand it myself, but I felt honored that God would choose us."

The teaching of Job on suffering is not contradictory to the doctrinal instruction of scripture on faith and victorious living, which is a great New Testament theme taught most profoundly by Paul. Yet, this same great Apostle Paul dealt with numerous hardships and persecutions. A very dramatic verse in his second letter to the Corinthians revealed the extreme suffering of the Apostle, "For we do not want you to be unaware brethren, of our affliction which came to us in Asia, that we were burdened excessively, beyond our strength, so that we despaired even of life" (2 Cor. 1:8, NASB). Such is the course of many heroes of faith. Paul himself also wrote in Romans 8:35-39:

> Who shall separate us from the love of Christ? shall tribulation, or distress, or persecution, or famine, or nakedness, or peril, or sword? As it is written, For thy sake we are killed all the day long; we are accounted as sheep for the slaughter. Nay, in all these things we are more than conquerors through him that loved us. For I am persuaded, that neither death, nor life, nor angels, nor principalities, nor powers, nor things present, nor things to come, Nor height, nor depth, nor any other creature, shall be able to separate us from the love of God, which is in Christ Jesus our Lord.

Without going into a complete exegesis of this passage, let me point out the phrase, which must not be overlooked. "Nay, in all these things…" Paul is saying, "Contrariwise …we are more than conquerors…" But, understand that it may be "in all these things." The word *in* is an excellent translation from the Greek word which is a preposition meaning a fixed position of place, time, or state. There is no question then that Paul is saying that as we suffer any or all the above events, **we are more than conquerors in that process. Hallelujah! We win!**

One of the most challenging concepts in the book of Job, especially in the light of the presence of evil, is God's culpability in Job's suffering. The same apostle, James, who spoke of the "patience of Job" (James 5:11), also wrote, "God cannot be tempted with evil, neither tempteth [H]e any man" (James 1:13b). Elsewhere in this writing is a brief and straightforward exegesis of this passage. Here we will compare it with Job. The emphasis will be on Job's words and a discussion of God's ultimate authority over *the Satan*. Job said that the "arrows of the Almighty" and the "terrors of God" were in him (6:4). Again, Job accused God of destroying him (10:8, 9). Similar statements are made in several other passages (16:11-14); 19:6-13; 27:2). I want to remind you that God did not deny these declarations, nor did He correct Job as He did the three friends (42:7-9).

The idea that God holds ultimate responsibility for Job's suffering is offensive in the view of many, but a brief survey of the facts of the two heavenly scenes will clarify the point. *The Satan* said, "Have [Y]ou not put a hedge about him, his household, and all that he has?" (1:10a, Hartley).[51] *Yahweh* responded, "Behold, everything that he has is in your power" (1:12a, Hartley).[52] The simple facts are God does bear ultimate responsibility because he lifted the "hedge" of His protection and gave *the Satan* authority over all Job had; and *the Satan* took that authority and either stole or destroyed all Job's possessions including his ten children. The one who brought the evil was in fact the "evil one" (John 17:15, NASB), but the permission for such evil action was in fact given by God Himself. Yet, there should be no attempt to make too much of God's responsibility for Job's suffering. **The permission or refusal to attack Job was in God's authority, and on both occasions, permission was given WITH LIMITATIONS.** The plan of attack and its implementation lay under *the Satan's* permitted and assigned authority.

The danger of trying to protect God's holiness and purity is that it moves one towards a dualism, which makes *the Satan* an equal but opposite to God. This kind of dualism is not a new doctrine. It was one of the earliest heresies of the Church. The error of this concept can be seen in this: there are not two eternals, God and evil, but only one Eternal, God! There are not two omnipotents, God and *the Satan,* but only one Omnipotent, God. Evil is the consequence coming from the created being, Lucifer, and his free choice in attempting to become as God. **In the book of Job, *the Satan* opposes God, but not as an equal, since he only operates by permission.**

In Job's story, there seems to be a kind of dual personality manifesting in God's actions. For example, in chapter twenty-seven verse two, Job says God has denied his rights and *Shaddai* has made his soul bitter. Do you see? **There is a reality to God's "other side" from which flow discipline, anger, wrath, and events like Job's innocent and undeserved suffering, which is totally unfathomable and therefore unexplainable.** We must trust and absolutely believe that His ways are still higher than man's ways (Isaiah 55:9).

Dwight Pryor, a personal friend of mine and a true scholar, responded to a request I made for help with Jewish sources for this project. Pryor, who recently passed on to his heavenly place in Christ, held a PhD, and he was one of the most intellectual of biblical scholars I personally know. He guest-lectured in top rabbinic circles in Jerusalem and elsewhere. His response is most appropriate to the point of

God's "other-ness." He stated, "As I see it, the ultimate challenge of the book of Job is not Job but God." He continued:

> It reminds me of C.S. Lewis' perceptive comment about Aslan at the end of The Lion, the Witch and the Wardrobe, "He's wild, you know. Not like a tame lion." There is an "untamed" side of God that the book of Job wrestles with. He will not always fit within our borders and boundaries, our logic and expectations. He is after all radically holy![53]

It is the radical holiness of God that causes us such confusing frustration when our unexplainable Job syndromes occur. The Job syndrome which Dale experienced in the story at the beginning of this chapter is a dramatic example of the unexplainable ways of God. Once again, **we are brought to the very precipice of unbelief as we face the mystery of our loving Father as He is allowing the fire of trial to purify our faith. This is not only a NECESSARY work in us, IT IS THE MOST NOBLE AND GOOD THING FATHER CAN DO FOR US.** I repeat a theme of this writing: His ways and thoughts are higher than ours!

MY PRAYER

Great God of all creation, Lord of the universe, the One and only God, I am humbled and instructed by Job's confidence in Your sovereignty. From my humanness, I long to be near Your presence. Help me now to trust that

You are doing a necessary work in me which is the very best thing for me. I need You to strengthen my faith as I yield my spirit to be baptized in Yours.

5
THE THEOLOGY OF THE BOOK OF JOB
PART TWO

> "Where then does wisdom come from?
>   Where does understanding dwell?
> It is hidden from the eyes of every living thing,
>   concealed even from the birds of the air.
> Destruction and Death say,
>   'Only a rumor of it has reached our ears.'
> God understands the way to it
>   and he alone knows where it dwells,
>   for he views the ends of the earth
>   and sees everything under the heavens.
> When he established the force of the wind
>   and measured out the waters,
>   when he made a decree for the rain
>   and a path for the thunderstorm,
> Then he looked at wisdom and appraised it;
>   he confirmed it and tested it.
> And he said to man,
>   'The fear of the Lord — that is wisdom,
>   and to shun evil is understanding.'"
>
> —Job 28:20-28 (NIV)

I do not remember the first time I saw Royce. He is a first cousin of mine who is my senior by enough that he became my hero when we were young. He was brave and athletic and could do so much that I could not do. Our lives have taken us down different paths, but we have one thing in common. We both have had a life-changing Job syndrome. I want to share the story of Royce and his wife, Marie.[54]

Royce and Marie had been worshipping and serving God for many years. Their marriage had brought two families together in a most unique way. I am telling their story as one Job syndrome, since that is what happened. They really suffered their trial together as one. Their story is all about faithfulness through some of the most intense life-threatening circumstances. Here is the beginning of that story as told by my cousin, Royce:

> We were working in the oil fields in a small town in Wyoming where we had drilled five new gas wells. We were turning them on to flow down the pipeline. A man went before us to clear everything and make sure things were okay. We had turned on four of them, and we started to turn on the last one. It was in a small building. There was enough gas in the building that when I turned the valve on to let the gas come up, the static electricity sparked, and the gas exploded. I was squatted in the door, and it knocked me out of the building. My son-in-law, Jaime, who worked with me, was in the building. At that time, I didn't know how he got out.
>
> I looked down, and my skin was burned, but I didn't know I was burned that bad. I couldn't stand up, because the explosion was so powerful. I began

to crawl on my hands and knees to get away from the building. I crawled maybe fifty feet or more before I could stand up. When I looked, my shirt was on fire, and my pants and belt was on fire. When I got that put out, I went back up to Jaime. I really didn't know what I was doing, but I think God was just guiding me up there. Somehow, we got in the truck. My hands were burned so bad that I couldn't drive, so Jaime drove out to the road. We were out in a pasture about a mile from the main road. He drove over the land. That was terrible!

When we got to the road, there was a policewoman there who put us in her car. Just as we were waiting for the ambulance, two off-duty EMT's came up who had water in their car. They put the water on us. The ambulance got there right away. We were only about a mile or two from the hospital. They laid Jaime down and I sat on the bench. I knew what was happening, but I couldn't feel a whole lot. I wasn't in pain. That was so amazing! They got us to the hospital and took me back…

Before all this happened earlier that morning, Marie was getting ready to go to work, and she turned on the TV while eating breakfast. A lady evangelist was on, and she was teaching on what to do in times of tragedy. She laid out steps to follow. Marie recalled, "I remember thinking that somebody is going to have a tragedy, and I will need to help them in some way." At that time, she had no inkling. She heard the sirens but had no idea it was Royce until she got the phone call. The evangelist laid out four steps. Marie said, "I only remember two now." They were, "Stay in the Word; and though it tarry, wait for it, because God has promised it." When she got the phone call, she still didn't think it was anything serious. There was no connection to what had been said. Marie said, "As I was hanging up from that call, Kathy, our daughter, called and said that Jaime was hurt, too. I left and went by just a couple of blocks away and picked her up, and we went to the hospital which was close." Here is Marie's account of what happened next:

> When I went in, I knew it was bad. The nurses just pointed the way. They had very concerned looks on their faces. I heard one of them say, "That's one of the wives." I went in, and Royce was sitting up. His skin was falling off. His eyebrows and eyelashes were burned off, and his hair was singed. His chest and back were bright red. They let me talk to him a minute. They said they had to intubate him [insertion of the tube for respiration], because his esophagus was swelling. They told him they would wait until I got there, since he would not be able to talk after inserting the tube. That was really scary, because it had been less than a year since Royce's brother, Neil, had died after he was put on a ventilator and he never came off. When they told us he needed the ventilator, Royce and I just looked at each other.
>
> They laid him down and asked me to leave while they did the procedure. I said, "Do you mind if I pray first?" They were really nice and said, "Of course," then stepped back...He was laying there hurt everywhere except his feet. So, I took hold of his feet, and the only prayer I prayed was, "Thank

You, God, that You are a healing God." They took me out in the hall, and while they were intubating him, a doctor talked to me. She kept saying, "If he survives, there will be multiple surgeries, and if he survives..." I asked if we were talking about life and death. She said that she really didn't believe my husband was going to make it. That's when the room just started spinning. I was standing there, and I could see her mouth moving, but after that, I didn't hear anything else.

Marie finally gathered herself together enough to go and check on Jaime. Royce was unbelievably calm because of shock. Jaime was the opposite. He was losing it. He was almost delirious. Jaime's burns were mostly second-degree burns, which were more painful. Royce's burns were deep enough to burn the nerves. Jaime's skin was bright red, while much of Royce's was white.

In a little while, she went back in to see Royce, and they asked her to sign the release forms. She recalled, "For the first time, I was aware of God's presence...It was the strangest feeling...like He took hold of me from the inside...It was a steadying, and all He said was, 'It will be okay.'" The meaning of "okay" was not clear, but she was encouraged to believe it.

Royce did not want to go on the ventilator, because of his memory of Neil dying after being ventilated. The anxiety about this was intense for both of them. The medical staff knew this was necessary, so they put him to sleep with the medication in order to intubate him. They prepared him for transport to a hospital capable of treating a burn patient.

The nearest burn unit was a small one in a town in Colorado. There were problems with the helicopters. They were unavailable. A decision was made to fly Royce and Jaime to a burn unit in Salt Lake City, Utah. They would have to jet them there. The two jets were two hours away. At first, Marie was not told what the final destination would be, because the medical staff did not know until the last minute; nor did she know she could ride with Royce in the jet until the Captain gave the okay just before takeoff. Ambulances carried them to the airport with Emergency Medical Technicians (EMTs) attending. The EMTs had to remove all dressings and redress everything before they could transport. The doctor had put in a police report that Royce would not survive the trip. Even with this report of a bleak prognosis, all throughout this process there were small miracles of Father's direction and provision, but these could only be seen in hindsight. At the time, there were only the whirlwind of activity and the stress in the gravity of Royce's condition.

I will not go into the details of the transport, except to relate this. Marie was sitting by herself and beginning to be a little sick from the stress and the movement of the airplane. God guided her thoughts to all the family and friends back home in Georgia and Florida who were by now praying for them. It started to be a real encouragement when the EMT behind her asked if she would like a soda. God sealed His presence and comfort in a refreshing drink!

Arriving in the big city, Royce was transported from the airport to the hospital by helicopter. Marie could then see Royce. She had not been able to see him in the airplane except his feet. She saw that during the flight, his face had turned black and his face and head were very swollen. In the hospital, Marie had difficulty keeping up with the EMTs getting him to the burn unit. When they arrived, she was asked to wait in the waiting room, and the big double doors closed in front of her. She stood there in the hallway all alone. There was not one person in sight. She found the waiting room, and in trying to collect herself, she called several of their children. Marie was experiencing the loneliness and isolation of a real Job syndrome.

One of the many blessings Marie recalled was how God provided a support network of family. She said, "Our daughter-in-law's mom drove all night from California and arrived pretty early the next day…Then, three of our children and two spouses arrived later that day, so within less than 24 hours of arriving we had our support group in place… From the get-go God surrounded us with praying people."

The next several days were very bad. Royce was kept unconscious, and the medical care for his burns was most severe. Even though he was in a drug-induced coma from his point of view, from the point of view of Marie and the medical staff, he could respond to instructions from the doctor like "move your leg." The drug they gave him helped him to forget much of his pain. But, when he was tied down and intubated, he would arch his back and scream in pain. Because of the tube, no sound came out of his mouth—only that awful scream from his soul. Marie said, "It was horrible." There was scraping (twice a day), washing, and medicating at least twice a day. Then there was a skin grafting surgery. The details of that procedure again are not necessary here. Amazingly, he only needed one surgery. From the beginning of his hospitalization, it was "touch and go" from one hour to the next.

Two days later, after the arrival of their children from Georgia, the doctors had a meeting with the family about Royce and Jaime. Their assessment of Royce's condition was grim. Marie asked, "When will he be out of danger?" The doctor responded, "When he walks out the door." In other words, there were no guarantees or optimism. There were three real threats to his survival: one, the danger of infection; two, the possibility of Acute Respiratory Distress Syndrome (ARDS) or pneumonia; and three, the possibility of heart failure. Once more, the often-used phrase Marie remembered hearing was, "If he lives…"

On the third day, Royce was to have his first surgery, because gangrene had set in. His heart had gone into a-fibrillation early that morning. Marie and Jaime's wife, Kathy, had been situated in a small apartment near the hospital. Upon getting this news, they quickly dressed and went to the hospital. Kathy called Robert and his wife in Georgia. These were friends for many years. Robert said, "I was up before daylight, and God gave me a scripture…" That scripture is Jeremiah 32:27, "Behold, I am the Lord, the God of all flesh: is there any thing too hard for me?"

The phrase "God of all flesh" immediately triggered faith. It became the promise, which sustained through that day's struggle and many more to come. Within a short time, Royce's heart returned to normal, and they were able to proceed to remove the gangrene skin. Once again, the God of all FLESH was moving one obstacle at a time. Marie said to herself, "You will not need flesh in heaven, so that means God is going to heal Royce's flesh here on earth."

I want to pause in the story and ask some pertinent questions. **Why not a total healing miracle all at once? **Why does God, our Father, sometimes only move in small increments? **We see He is moving during those times, but He is not delivering totally. This kind of Job syndrome tries both patience and faith to a breaking point.** The "why" questions ultimately remain mostly unanswered. **We still move forward one step at a time—by faith!**

They diagnosed Royce as having burns over 46% of his body from his waist up. He had second and third degree burns over his chest, face, arms, hands, and back. The right hand was more severely burned than the left, and the wrist had fourth degree burns. He was asleep (drug induced) for five weeks. When they finally allowed him to wake up, he began to experience his own pain. He remembered, "I couldn't do anything...It was the hardest thing I've ever been through." He could not talk. The tube had to be left in because of concern for the development of ARDS (lung failure). Royce had very anxious moments when mucous in the airway made it hard to breathe. He said, "I couldn't talk...they still had my hands tied down, and I couldn't even get anyone's attention."

When they would do the baths twice a day, which took as much as two hours, they would paralyze him, so that he would not flinch and move. They were literally removing the injured skin. Although he was on heavy painkillers and temporarily paralyzed, there was still an enormous amount of pain. He couldn't move or turn. They only put some gauze on him. They kept the room very warm so that he would not feel so cold. Royce's physical misery was truly extreme!

For seven and a half weeks, Royce was hospitalized. Then there were many weeks of rehabilitation. In fact, even after moving back to Georgia, the rehabilitation went on for about a year. There were many other details of his excruciating recovery process. These have been written in a book, which they have published since his recovery.

As in Job's syndrome, Royce and Marie experienced a multi-pronged attack. There were work related problems for Royce and Jaime. Some people who were supposed to be very close showed anger that things were not done like they thought would be best. There was a vicious verbal attack which was demonic.

Then, one night two young men who had also been in a gas explosion were brought in the unit next to Royce. Marie did not know what was going on, but she sensed the spirit of death (a very real revelation of the presence of death) and began to walk around Royce's room praying for protection. The next morning, she found out the two men had passed about the time she was praying.

Royce had not looked in a mirror for five and a half weeks. He began to have depressive thoughts about what he would look like. He prayed, "Father, I would rather You take me now rather than leave me here as a monster." The Holy Spirit began to cause him to think about the Apostle John and even gave him dreams about John. At that time, they did not know that history records the Apostle was boiled in oil, but did not die, so he was sent to Patmos where he received the Revelation of Jesus Christ. John talked to Royce in his dreams. Later, Marie asked him about what John said in those visits. Royce couldn't tell her. He could only describe how he felt a calming, a peacefulness, and that John's message was too wonderful to talk about. After those "visitations" from John, there was some strength to continue the fight for life.

Royce's lungs eventually did go into failure (ARDS). At that point, the respirator was doing the breathing for him. This day was the most critical day on several fronts. Royce immediately went from a probability of dying to almost a certainty of dying. When the doctor left the room after telling them the diagnosis, he looked at Marie and said, "I'm so sorry." Royce and Marie both were thinking this was a death sentence, since two of his older brothers had died from ARDS. Later that day, a respiratory specialist told Marie, "If his lungs do not heal themselves, he will not make it." It was that night in their most profound crisis when Royce's God-event happened. Here is the amazing story of the supernatural intervention as he remembered it:

Early on, after we were in the hospital, Marie had called Trish, our daughter-in-law, and told her to call one of our closest church friends, because "I think she's got a word for us." Before Trish could call, the friend called and said, "I have a word for you." She gave us Hebrews 11:1, "Now faith is the substance of things hoped for, the evidence of things not seen." That night Marie was praying that as a prayer over me, because my lungs had just quit. It was total ventilator. She was praying that over and over, until she got so sleepy, she sat down in a chair and went to sleep. That's the night Jesus came. He didn't say anything...He was just standing there, and the room got so-o-o clean. The first thing I wanted to do...I probably tried to get out of the bed...I wasn't tied down then. I just wanted to get on the floor, you know? ...That's what caused me to not like that song anymore that says, "...and I find myself standing (in His presence)..." When we get in front of Him, He's going to be so clean, we won't be able to stand up! That's the way I felt...He came to me and just washed me, and it cleansed me...I had never been that clean before in my entire life. With the burns, that's the last thing I would have wanted, a washing, but He washed me so I could come up. I couldn't have come up before He cleansed me. Then, I started to rise up off the bed...

I came up off the bed...I'm not sure of it, but I know I did. I came off the bed, and I looked down...it was so ugly down here, and our world is ugly right now. It was clean up there, and I didn't want to go back down on that bed. I believe I was having an out-of-body experience.

When He washed me, I was finally able to talk

to Him. I couldn't even speak before then…I couldn't speak! I said, "If You don't heal me, I'm gonna die." You know? I knew I was. Jesus said, "Royce…" And, I mean He called my name! "…I have heard their prayers, and My love will lift you up." Later, I got to thinking on that. What He said was much more powerful than healing. He said, "My love will lift you up." After that day, I started getting better. In less than two weeks, in fact, it was ten days; I was out of that hospital!

Royce's recuperation surprised all the medical staff. There was so much to do in removing the ventilator, removing the plug in the tracheotomy, teaching him to talk, teaching him to eat, and continuing to dress the skin. He had lost 50 pounds. He began to walk and get exercise. It is humorous that after five and a half weeks the first words he spoke were, "Don't ever put me in that chair again, it's killing my back!"

As with Job, when Jesus came to Royce, there was a restoration of spirit and a wonderful peace. There were still physical hurdles, pain, and discomfort, but there was "no fear."

To this day, Royce must exercise and care for his grafted skin. There are no sweat glands or oil glands in that skin. He must keep moisturizers on those areas. He experiences extreme cold and heat. God worked a real miracle for his face. Unless one looks very closely, there are no noticeable scars. His lips still bother him, so he must be careful eating. He doesn't literally walk with a limp, but he carries his marks. They are badges of courage and faith.

I know you may be thinking, "What about Jaime?" Jaime suffered his own Job syndrome at the same time as Royce and Marie. He was injured severely but not as severely as Royce. His hospital stay was not nearly as lengthy as Royce's either. Here is a part of that story Marie shared with me:

> Jaime suffered greatly from survivor's guilt. He was the engineer in charge and his father-in-law was hanging between life and death. After his release, when he was able to see Royce for the first time in the hospital, he had to be led away. He then collapsed in sobs. This was very out of character for that Wyoming man. It was a powerful breaking… Our son-in-law had a three-day encounter with God when he was first released from the hospital. It was an awesome time for him. He came away from that with the same revelation that God says, "Thus far and no farther!"

When I asked Royce and Marie if they had developed a "life message," Marie was quick to answer. **Her greatest revelation was that God "is my friend."** This came to her in Utah when the circumstance was the most difficult. Out of that revelation, she said, **"No matter what comes to us, if we can open up to it, and embrace it, and trust Him in it, we will find things in Him you can't find but in the darkness."** She began to talk about "treasures of the darkness," which comes from the writings of Isaiah.

> And I will give thee the treasures of darkness, and hidden riches of secret places, that thou mayest know that I, the Lord, which call thee by thy name, am the God of Israel.
>
> -Isaiah 45:3

Marie continued, "I think there are places in Him and revelations of His love and His greatness that you can only find by going in those dark places with Him." **I am convinced this truth is at least a partial answer to the question quoted from Job at the beginning of this chapter. From where do wisdom and understanding come, since it is hidden from every living thing? Much of it only comes from the darkness in the hidden and secret places.**

As with all the other interviews, I asked Royce and Marie, "Have you ever discovered why all this happened to you?" To my surprise, Royce said, "Yes, I think I know why...It was because **it was the worst thing that ever happened to me, but it was the best thing that ever happened to me...it was the best thing."**

Once again, we see that God's ways are mysterious, and sometimes they do not make sense to the natural mind. **We must press ourselves to learn of Him, Who He is, and how much He cares.** It is to this quest for God that I want to continue the discussion of the theology of the book of Job. **As we come to know ABOUT HIM, by His Spirit, may we come to KNOW HIM.**

The Theology of Job

The theology of the book of Job is so deep and philosophical that it can be overwhelming. It can be seen in almost every aspect of the story: man's relationship to God as a worshipper; *the Satan's* relationship to God as a subservient spirit; God the Creator and Lord; and, ultimately, God as the merciful benefactor returning Job to a place in his society with twice the glory of his earlier position. Perhaps, as with Job, Royce and Marie, and the other examples in this book, we can never truly appreciate God's goodness until we experience the darkness, in fact, the evil, which has come from the evil one, *the Satan*. There are figures, which represent evil in the book of Job and should be noted and understood, since they greatly affected Job without his knowledge until God clarified the facts. The names of these figures are known in some of the extra-biblical Mesopotamian and Canaanite literature. They are *Rahab* and *Leviathan*. Hartley stated, "[T]hese creatures symbolize the forces of chaos in opposition to God."[55] A third creature, *Behemoth*, is exclusive to the Bible and only has two references outside of Job (Ps. 73:22; Isa. 30:6) where *Behemoth* is translated "beast" or "beasts." **Together, these three symbols represent the forces of evil, which are constantly at work in every Job syndrome. By exposing these personalities, God is uncovering the very nature and methodologies of these figures as they create the chaos of the Job syndromes, which so devastatingly affect us.**

Rahab

The two references to *Rahab* speak of God's sovereignty over, and His destruction of this ruling sea monster (Job 9:13, 26:12; NIV) (*Rahab* does not appear in KJV). She is referenced in similar terms in Psalm 89:11 and Isaiah 51:9-10. Two other references to *Rahab* have this evil force symbolizing Egypt (Psa. 87:4; Isa. 30: 7). In the *Apokalupsis* (Rev. 17:1-18:3), there is the depiction of the "great prostitute" who sits on many waters. This could well be the final scene of this *Rahab*, the ruling creature over the sea. The angel speaking to John in the Revelation interpreted the scene, "The waters you saw, where the prostitute sits are peoples, multitudes, nations and languages" (Rev. 17:15, NIV). So, the sea represents people, and the prostitute bears the title, "MYSTERY BABYLON," which symbolizes great confusion or chaos. It is more than a slight likelihood that she represents a world-influencing religious system as she also rides a beast who symbolizes a political or governmental system, which is against Christ.

If these interpretations are valid, we may conclude that the subtle religious confusion introduced to tempt Job to deny truth and faith to follow a system expounded by his comforters, has become, in the last days, a worldwide religious system deceiving the masses to worship in idolatry. **This *Rahab* influence is a primary source of the Christian hedonism (I know that is an oxymoron) that is affecting so much of the postmodern Evangelical church world with its emphasis on self,**

which is idolatry. The allurement of *Rahab* is a constant threat to true faith in God as it promises peace through religious works. Job faced a similar crisis of self-absorption and false theology. The religious confusion that Job had begun to experience in the well-intentioned advice of his comforters was in fact laying a trap for Job so that *Rahab's* cohort, *the Satan*, might win his challenge to God. **Such is the case in every Job syndrome. The Rahab effect takes place when religious confusion is experienced to the point of frustrating faith.**

When one is suffering an unmerited trial and feeling the extreme pain either emotionally, physically or both, there is often a strong temptation to doubt the promises of God. This is the source of the confusion between what is real or true in the Word, and what is not true. At the least, it is perceived that way in one's state of mind when it seems God is nowhere to be found. We tend to ask questions like, "Is what I've been taught the truth? Am I losing my faith? Where is the God of love and mercy Whom I have been serving faithfully?" **In other words, our faith is tried to the breaking point. That is the raw agony of the Job syndrome, a "trial of faith."** The threat to our theological perspective can bring such bewilderment and perplexity that the only way out seems to be to "curse God and die."

Once again, Job is the paragon of faithfulness in spite of *Rahab's* attempt to bring him to utter uncertainty. It is to Job's credit that he recognized *Rahab's* potential danger and expressed his confidence that God overrules her. This is expressed in Job chapters 9 and 26:

> God does not restrain his anger;
> even the cohorts of Rahab cowered at his feet.
> -Job 9:13 (NIV)

> By his power he churned up the sea;
> by his wisdom he cut Rahab to pieces.
> -Job 26:12 (NIV)

There is no doubt that the influence of *Rahab* is destructive on the large scale of the Church world. On a personal level, it can wreak the same havoc. It is so important to understand the ways of deception of this monster over the sea of humanity in order to identify the nature of the personal attacks in a Job syndrome.

Behemoth

The creature *Behemoth* may be the most controversial entity of the Book of Job. First, there is the question of the beast's natural or biological reality. Commentators cover the spectrum from natural reality and only natural reality, to reality plus mythical, to mythical only, and on to allegorical interpretation. Over approximately three hundred years of modern interpretation, the majority of those seeing a natural animal believe *Behemoth* to be a hippopotamus. The name *Behemoth* in the Hebrew is the plural of ordinary domestic animals and is suggestive of a natural creature. On the other hand, the form of the word is the feminine plural used as a masculine singular, and it seems to indicate something different. It is this difference that I want to address as we come to a new understanding of this symbolic figure. Those who hold the interpretation of hippopotamus must deal with several descriptive incompatibilities, which are usually done by invoking hyperbole and poetic license to maintain the identification.

The beast *Behemoth* and his habitat do not describe an animal that can easily be identified (Job 40:15-24). The beast as described is not a predator but an herbivore. He is not equipped for offense, but he is extremely well equipped for defense. He dwells in the marsh and even in the hills. Pay close attention to this description:

> Look at the *behemoth*, [Italics mine]
>   which I made along with you
>   and which feeds on grass like an ox.
> What strength he has in his loins,
>   what power in the muscles of his belly!
> His tail sways like a cedar;
>   the sinews of his thighs are close-knit.
> His bones are tubes of bronze,
>   his limbs like rods of iron.
> He ranks first among the works of God,
>   yet his Maker can approach him with his sword.
>   -Job 40:15-19 (NIV)

None other than the enigmatic Dr. Wolfers delineated the best interpretation of *Behemoth* appropriate to this writing. To begin, Wolfers discussed the two passages that used the word *Behemoth* outside of the book of Job (Ps. 73:22; Isa. 30:6).[56] In the Authorized Version, both of these instances of *Behemoth* are translated as "beast" (Ps. 73:22) and "beasts" (Isa. 30:6). In Psalm 73:22, the Psalmist admitted to God, "I was senseless and ignorant; / I was a brute beast before you" (NIV). This confession of a *Behemoth* nature is significant. In Isaiah 30:6, Isaiah was prophesying God's message to Judah, "the oracle concerning the beasts of the Negev" (NASB). This was a description of the "rebellious" people of Judah (Isa. 30:9, 12). In both cases then, **Behemoth was the beast within people.** The poet Asaph and the prophet Isaiah are describing the nature of humans as a beast nature. It should be noted that evolutionists explain this beast nature away as the result of the process of evolving from animals. That explanation is an excuse making it too easy to declare innocence for beastly behavior. Wolfers' exegesis of Job 40:15 lead to an unusual conclusion. Concerning the phrase "*Behemoth* (italics mine) which I made with you," He stated, "The real meaning, I suggest is 'fashioned as your other half,' hence 'molded with your clay'."[57] This dedicated scholar believed the use of **Behemoth is God's description of fallen human nature.** If Wolfers was correct (he did trump the hippopotamus idea), then a brief review of the Pauline usage of "flesh" is necessary to complete the image of *Behemoth*.

God said of *Behemoth* that only "his maker can approach him with [H]is sword" (Job 40:19b), which indicates **man cannot control or destroy this beast. Behemoth, the beast in every person, is the same as the "flesh" principle laid out in Romans and**

Galatians. Paul, by the Spirit, wrote, that there is no condemnation to those "who walk not after the flesh (Gr. *sarx*), but after the Spirit" (Rom. 8:1). Again, Paul stated, "For to be carnally (Gr. *sarkos*) minded is death; but to be spiritually minded is life and peace. Because the carnal (Gr. *sarkos*) mind is enmity against God: for it is not subject to the law of God, neither indeed can be" (Rom.8: 6-7). **The "flesh,"** ***Behemoth*****, is God's enemy and therefore against any obedient and loving service to Him by the believer. The problem with modern believers, as with Job's** ***Behemoth*****, is that only God can strike him with His sword, which is His Word.** Paul confirmed that it is only through the Spirit that the deeds of the "flesh" can be mortified (Rom. 8:13). Habel implied a similar interpretation of *Behemoth* and Job when he stated, "*Behemoth* (italics mine) and Job have a common origin and their destinies are bound up together in some way."[58]

It is fascinating to me that this beast nature is the very thing evolutionists have observed. They rationalize that because this nature is observable and because there are many biological similarities, we must have indeed evolved from the lower species at some point. I will not go into a discussion of creationism versus evolutionism here. There are many excellent sources, which deal with that subject. As a Bible-believing Christian, I will only point out that God Himself said, "…*behemoth*, which I made with you…" We are the creation of God, and He made us with the "flesh" nature. That nature, which was pure and innocent in Adam before his rebellious disobedience, became the beast, the

Behemoth, in Adam and all his progeny in the Fall. As the spirit man died in Adam, the "flesh" began its reign and dominance. **We all have the beast, the "flesh." Without the "sword" of God, this nature dominates and controls our lives. Using a Job syndrome is, in fact, one of the ways God works to control the *Behemoth* within us.** My advice is to yield to His "sword" as it chops away at your *Behemoth*.

The apostle Paul put it this way:

> For they that are after the flesh do mind the things of the flesh; but they that are after the Spirit the things of the Spirit. For to be carnally minded is death; but to be spiritually minded is life and peace. Because the carnal mind is enmity against God: for it is not subject to the law of God, neither indeed can be. So then they that are in the flesh cannot please God.
>
> -Romans 8:5-8

Paul again summed it up beautifully in Galatians 5:16, "This I say then, Walk in the Spirit, and ye shall not fulfil the lust of the flesh." The truth to Job, as it is also to us, cannot be other than this: unless God controls the *Behemoth* within us, it will do as it pleases.

Leviathan

The third and final figure in Job, which is in fact a personification of evil, is seen in the image of *Leviathan*. **Understanding *Leviathan*, as he is described in the**

final speech of *Yahweh* (Job 42:1-34), is a major key to understanding the entire book of Job and, therefore, the Job syndrome. Dr. Fyall covered the *Leviathan* passages extensively, including those outside of Job. He stated, "[T]he *Leviathan* (italics mine) passages raise in most acute form the problem of the relationship of God to evil and the underlying question of creation."[59]

The problem of God's relationship to evil is indeed the larger problem of Job, even larger than that of divine retribution or justice, for it is foundational to both of the former. The final phrase of Fyall's observation gives cause for second thoughts. Creation is not, in and of itself, a question, a problem, or a cause of a problem. When God created all, He called it "good" (Gen. 1:31). The "Fall" (used as the common theological term) of man and the curses that followed are the causes of the observable wrongs and violence in nature (Gen. 3, cf. Rom. 8:22). To ignore the consequences of man's disobedience in Adam is to ignore the entrance of evil, both moral and physical, into the world of man. We sinned in Adam and Eve. We talked to the snake. Our disobedience brought evil into the world.

As to an understanding of *Leviathan*, following some of the parallel passages outside of Job is an absolute necessity for comprehensive exegesis. The following passages in Job and outside of Job are discussed in order to draw conclusions as to the identity of *Leviathan*, who has a number of personal titles and names in scripture.

The first mention of *Leviathan* in the book of Job did not mention him by that name, but it identified him by a title, which described one of his major functions. In Job 1:6, at the first of two scenes in the heavenly court, *the Satan* appeared before God. He fulfilled his character and position as the accuser when he charged that Job only served God for the blessings he received. *The Satan* did not appear before God as the serpentine dragon of Job 41. He was there in his office as a cherub, one of the "sons of God" (Hebrew, *bene ha Elohim*)[60] who must account for his activities. The second mention of *Leviathan* (Job 2:1, 2) is similar to the first and under the follow-up circumstances to the first. Again, *the Satan* was the antagonist debating with God over Job, and he was still functioning as an angelic being, however a fallen one.

The third mention of *Leviathan* comes from a most pained and urgent cry of Job, "May those who curse days curse that day, / those who are ready to rouse *Leviathan* (italics are mine)" (3:8, NIV). The name *Leviathan* does not appear in the Authorized Version, but it is supported by most modern English versions. It is, in fact, in the Hebrew text. Within this reference, the name that is associated with several extra-biblical legends (found in certain Mesopotamian documents of antiquity) was spoken by Job in a wish to have his birthday reversed and obliterated by the powerful sea monster who is supposed to have that kind of ability. **The sinister forces of evil were being felt as a presence by Job.** For example, in 7:1-15, he lamented that when he tried to rest, his dreams and visions were frightening, even terrifying. Job said he would rather be strangled to death than to live like that (7:15). Not having the revelation of

Leviathan, his real enemy, as in chapter 41, Job assumed that *El Shaddai* (6:4) was responsible for his torment. In chapter 41, following immediately the discussion of *Behemoth*, God described *Leviathan*, and He asked Job questions, which exposed Job's total inability to deal with this creature.

A brief word about a literal zoological explanation of these creatures is appropriate. The usual and often repeated interpretations of hippopotamus and crocodile or elephant and whale are simply unsatisfactory. Poetic license notwithstanding, the discrepancies of description and biological facts are simply too great to be ignored. An alternative view assumed by a few others is very interesting but un-provable. They see the eagles of 39:27-30 to be the now pre-historic raptors, and that *Behemoth* and *Leviathan* are describing dinosaurs, which might have been living in Job's day. The theory that there were still dinosaurs living in Job's day is more debatable at a scientific level. Whether these creatures had a literal existence concurrently with Job or not is of little consequence for interpretive purposes. What was of great importance to Job and to the modern believer is the meaning of their symbolisms. Concerning *Leviathan* Hartley wrote, "The poetic description reveals that the author skillfully weaves into the portrait of an earthly serpentine animal the features of a mythical dragon. The implication of *Yahweh's* (italics mine) questioning is that Job could not master this earthly creature, let alone its cosmic counterpart."[61]

Leviathan is the creature who historically has been the embodiment of the chaotic forces of evil. Three references outside of Job show different characteristics. First, in Psalm 74:14, *Leviathan* was defeated by *Yahweh* in the person of Pharaoh and the destruction of his army. The defeat was notably in the sea, which symbolizes rebellious humanity, which stands against God. Second, in Psalm 104:26, *Leviathan* was described as frolicking or sporting in the sea; once again it symbolized *Leviathan's* power over sinful humanity. Finally, in Isaiah 27, *Leviathan's* end will come as this eschatological prophecy predicts, "In that day, the Lord will punish with [H]is sword, [H]is fierce, great and powerful sword, *Leviathan* (italics mine) the gliding serpent, *Leviathan* (italics mine) the coiling serpent; [H]e will slay the monster of the sea" (Isa. 27:1, NIV).

A review of scriptural references to *Leviathan* in his several personas will show the development, or more precisely, the degenerative evolution of this creature. **ced *Leviathan's* first appearance in scripture was in Genesis 3:1 where his guise was that of a seemingly harmless and beguiling serpent.** His influence was such that man disobeyed God and plunged the whole of creation into a state of groaning and travailing while awaiting its redemption by Jesus Christ (Rom. 8:21-22). **When God unmasked *the Satan* of Job 1 and 2 in chapter 41, he was the not-so-attractive *Leviathan*, a creature who struck fear into the hearts of those who had the revelation. He already had the characteristics of the mature and powerful dragon he would become.** Isaiah described the pre-history position of this creature. In Isaiah 14:12-15 (within a prophecy against the King of Babylon), he was called "**the morning star, son of the dawn**" (NIV) showing his exalted position among the heavenly creatures before he was "cast down to the earth." Jesus Christ Himself took up this imagery in Luke 10:18 when He declared, "I beheld Satan as lightning fall from heaven." Again, the pre-history character and nature as well as the rebellion and heavenly ejection of this personage were the subject of a parallel prophecy to the Isaiah passage in Ezekiel (28:12-19) over the King of Tyrus. He was called the "**anointed cherub**," and he was the most beautiful of God's creatures. But, his pride prompted rebellion against God. In fact, this prophecy includes his original boast:

> In the pride of your heart
>   you say, "I am a god;
> I sit on the throne of a god
>   in the heart of the seas."
>
> -Ezekiel 28:2 (NIV)

The desire to "be like God" (NASB and other modern English versions) is the very same sin with which *the Satan* tempted Eve in the Garden of Eden. In this unique passage, Ezekiel preached that this "anointed cherub" had "been in Eden the garden of God," the very place of Adam's temptation. A most interesting feature of this prophecy is that this creature's ability to produce fire from within will be the instrument of his destruction (cf. Job 41:19-21 and Ezek. 28:12-19).

The last descriptions of this creature in Job 41 is found in the book of the Revelation. The references in this book are too involved to cover in this writing, but a brief discussion of a few references is necessary to the finalized identity of *Leviathan*. In Revelation 2:9, the suffering church of Smyrna was in great conflict with a false religious system called the "synagogue of Satan." Once again, this is the traditional religious system similar to that of Job's comforters who gave advice that would have led Job to failure and sin. The church of Pergamos, a church seriously divided by false doctrine, was located where Satan's "seat" or "throne" was (Rev. 2:13). In Thyatira, the church was reeling under the influence of Jezebel who had led some into the "depths of Satan" (Rev. 2:24). The church at Philadelphia, of which no complaint was pronounced, had the same conflict with false religion as Smyrna. They were opposed by another "synagogue of Satan" (Rev. 3:9). What an amazing fact! Four out of seven of the churches addressed had direct conflicts with *Satan* through false religion bringing deception.

Based on the interpretations drawn from the discussions above, the following track to *Leviathan's* final identity and destruction is offered. In Revelation 12:3-10, a red dragon is described as leading a revolt in heaven which has a drastic, even cosmic result, "[H]e was cast out into the earth; and his angels ("the third part," verse 4) were cast out with him" (verse 9b). In verse 10, this personage is identified as "the accuser of the brethren," which matches the title of *the Satan* in Job 1 and 2. **In Revelation 10:9, the identity of *Leviathan* is summarized for all the biblical references, "And the great dragon (*Leviathan*) was** cast out, that old serpent (of the Garden of Eden), called the Devil (the tempter of Jesus Christ), and Satan (Job's accuser and antagonist), which deceiveth the whole world." The identity of *Leviathan* is clear. For those commentators who have declared a problem because *the Satan* of the prologue does not appear in the epilogue, perhaps they should consider that he has appeared in the final speech of God in chapter 41 unmasked to reveal that he is one and the same as *Leviathan*.

God revealed to Job who his real enemy was, and that only *Yahweh's* relational love and protection would shield and safeguard him from the dragon of evil. Job had experienced first-hand the capabilities of his non-human enemy. Now he also understood that although God had ultimate responsibility for allowing the tragic events of his life, *Yahweh* had kept him from *the Satan's* desire to kill him. In other words, God had saved him from *Leviathan's* final death-dealing blow.

Salvation is, in fact, God's ultimate plan and priority for all of us. Constantly, we need our Father to save us from *Leviathan's* plans to deceive and destroy us both physically and spiritually. The New Testament teaches clearly that salvation is only obtained through faith:

> For I am not ashamed of the gospel of Christ: for it is the power of God unto salvation to every one that believeth; to the Jew first, and also to the Greek. For therein is the righteousness of God revealed from

faith to faith: as it is written, The just shall live by faith.

-Romans 1:16-17

For God hath not appointed us to wrath, but to obtain salvation by our Lord Jesus Christ...

-1 Thessalonians 5:9

How shall we escape, if we neglect so great salvation; which at the first began to be spoken by the Lord, and was confirmed unto us by them that heard him...

-Hebrews 2:3

And I heard a loud voice saying in heaven, Now is come salvation, and strength, and the kingdom of our God, and the power of his Christ: for the accuser of our brethren is cast down, which accused them before our God day and night.

-Revelation 12:10

The foreshadowing of this New Testament idea of salvation through faith had dawned on Job, and so, in *Yahweh's* presence along with an understanding of His explanations, Job was content. Perhaps at this point you and I would like to stop Job and say, "Job, why don't you use this opportunity to ask this God of the whirlwind those questions you asked before which He hasn't answered, especially that 'why' question." But, profoundly**, the questions of Job's theological mindset have been answered, or they were no longer of any consequence. Job rested in his spirit even though at the time of the God-encounter, he still had the loathsome disease and** none of the restoration blessings had even begun. His "salvation" was only spiritual in that moment as he still lived under the plague of evil, but he continued to trust and worship in the very presence of *Yahweh*, the God of the whirlwind.

MY PRAYER

Lord of the universe, Almighty God, sovereign King of kings, Daddy, I am only one in the great "sea" of humanity. I clearly recognize my enemy, *Leviathan*, the chaos monster who presides over the "sea." Since You, and You alone, have power and authority over this enemy of mine, I ask that You continue to authorize and empower me as I rebuke and resist my Accuser. I also see the revelation of my flesh as the "beast" within me, which is opposed to You. Wield the sword of Your Word against every carnal thing, which continues in trying to rule over my thoughts, concerns, emotions, attitudes, and affections. My only hope is Your speedy answer to this desperate petition: DADDY, SAVE ME!

6
CONCLUSIONS TOWARD SOLUTIONS

Then Job answered the Lord,
   I know that You can do all things
      And that no purpose of Yours can be thwarted.
You have said,
   "Who is this that hides My plan without knowledge?"
      Indeed, I have spoken without understanding,
   Of things too wonderful for me which I did not grasp.
"Hear, and I will speak;
   I will ask you, and do you inform Me."
I have heard of You by hearsay,
   but now my own eyes have seen You.
Therefore I abase myself
   And repent in dust and ashes.
                              -Job 42:1-6 (Gordis)[62]

    The questions of what and why concerning the great trial of the innocent and righteous Job are as much unanswered today as they were when the book was written. Any person going through the Job syndrome will continue to ask Job's questions, because they have been left unanswered intentionally by the Holy Spirit and His Job writer for the personal discovery of the sufferer in his or her own encounter with God. Each one experiencing the Job syndrome must ultimately see what Job saw in the above passage and submit to *Yahweh*, as did Job. Each person traveling Job's path, after finding out, at least in part, the "what" of their tragic circumstances (from their medical doctor, financial investor, lawyer, or other advisor) will immediately turn to God and ask the more subjective questions. **It is human nature. We cannot help ourselves. We think we must know an answer to the "why" question.** At this point, I must ask a question of my own, "Why are people so incessantly curious?" David Burrell observed this behavior and stated, "There is, of course, a simple human answer: we all get tired of waiting in incomprehension, so must suitably explain things, first to ourselves, so that we can go on."[63] And so, going on, we still ask our many questions. Looking at God's speech to Job, I believe that *Yahweh* is not offended by our questioning any more than He was with Job's. In fact, He may be amused (if that is not a too human description).

When a life-experience has an origin, like Job's, in the beyond-human and incomprehensible eternal will of God, all attempts to understand or explain are going to fall extremely short of satisfactory. Sufferers, and the ministers who try to help them, especially stumble over the concepts of retribution and fair justice, because, most of the time, they are laden with false assumptions in their Christian world-view. Gordis, a Jewish professor, still recognized the problem when he wrote, "Any view of the universe that pretends to explain it fully is, by that very token, untrue."⁶⁴ **There must be a sense in which the ways of God remain awesomely mysterious and not subject to human explanation, or else He is not God.**

I want to share an example of God's incomprehensible will. This is the story of the Job syndrome of my friend, Sarah. This trial of her faith, and ultimately the turning point of her life, I will share in her own words:

> With things going my way, I was happy as a lark. It was harvest time, and I always took off from college to help with the harvest. Our Midwestern farm had about 3,000 acres of corn. It was busy but happy times, because it always held hope. It was a cool day and a rain had sent us home early. My mother had picked up our oldest son, Jack, from school, and she had our two-year-old, Timothy. I usually had the children with me in the truck, but it was a rare occasion. Mother wanted to take Timothy with her visiting, and that is why she had him with her that evening.
>
> After we got the corn in, my husband and I headed to pick up Timothy and eat dinner. Mother was taking Jack to the doctor the next day for me, so he stayed with her. By the time we finished with dinner, it was turning dark outside, so we headed home to get ready for the next day. Our days started well before daylight. This night was like any other night in my country life. As we pulled up to the front door, I reminded my husband that we had not gone through the front door that day, so it still had the chain lock on. We lived out in the middle of "nowhere" in a corn field. Our door had

three locks. He backed up and drove around to the back of the house. We were talking and collecting our things. Mother had sent empty bowls back from a previous meal, and we had the baby's things, the usual items. Timothy had fallen asleep on my husband's shoulder. It was a time before child-seats. He never woke up as my husband got out of the truck with him. I collected the blanket, bag, and plastic dishes upon getting out of the truck. While I was dilly-dallying around, he walked on up to the house and opened the back door with Timothy in his arms. Timothy still had his head on his dad's shoulder.

 I was about three feet from the door when my husband flipped the light switch on by the door. As the light pierced the darkness, I lifted my head to witness my life changing forever. I saw a man step from behind the door to my husband's back. Then I watched as the man hit him so hard that he fell to his knees. Jesus gave him the power to jump up and swing around to kick the man backwards. I started screaming for him to run; he still had Timothy in his arms. He tried to set Timothy down, but he wouldn't stand. Then he turned to run as I saw the man step in the doorway and start shooting. As I watched in slow motion, I heard my husband's footsteps crunch on the gravel and cross the highway, which ran in front of our house. I sighed in relief that he had gotten away with the baby. As I stood there frozen, the intruder turned his attention to me. He looked me in the eyes, and I knew I was in trouble. My first thought was to beg him not to shoot me, but as clear as I ever heard anything, the God of the universe spoke to me. He said, "There is no mercy there."

I lifted up my arms to God like a child. I replied, "Then You help me." At that moment, he fired the gun. The impact spun me around and it seemed like it took fifteen minutes for me to fall. As I was falling, God was talking. He told me, "The man thinks he has killed you. You are going to fall face down and I am going to stop you from breathing. Don't move because I am with you." Just as God said, the guy was sure I was dead. The bullet had entered the flesh at my forearm and traveled past my elbow, entering and splitting my arm bone [humerus] stopping before it got to my shoulder. I heard the gun click again but he was out of rounds. He stepped over me twice to steal the meager belongings of a young couple, and then he left. As soon as I heard the car tires on the gravel driveway from our barn, I jumped up running through the house. I arrived on the front porch screaming for my husband to answer me. If the guy had looked back, he would have seen me, because I was on the porch before he got out of sight. When there was no answer from my husband, I "lost it" for a second. Then he called out from the darkness and told me to call for help. I ran back inside to call his parents who were our closest neighbors for several miles.

Father never left us in the days that followed. His grace surrounded us as we buried our two-year-old from a head injury and gunshot wound. Our physical injuries were minimal, but our lives and souls would never be the same. As my husband ran through the house to get away, we were not alone. As he touched the door lock to escape, the door just popped open with a deadbolt, a chain lock and locked door handle. The forensic team from the city nearby never found one bullet in the house although he had emptied the gun chamber of eight rounds. The last round was used on me. There were angels in our house that night. I have faced much difficulty since then but never alone. His grace is sufficient for me.[65]

When I interviewed Sarah, because I thought her story was important for this writing, I asked her to continue from the point of calling for help. Here is the rest of the Job Syndrome of this real saint.

She then went to the front steps and called for her husband. At first, he did not respond, because he thought it might be a trick. Sarah began to lose any control she had up to that moment. He then stepped out of the darkness and came up the steps. That is when Sarah saw that Timothy's blond head was wounded. She did not know then that it was from two injuries. As she saw her baby's condition, she began to fall apart. Sarah managed to call her father-in-law. Since they lived only two miles away, her father-in-law and husband's brother arrived almost immediately. They all got in the car and proceeded to the hospital. Sarah's father-in-law had brought a shotgun not realizing that the intruder-murderer had already gone.

The car was a smaller sports model. Timothy's dad was sitting in the back with the baby still in his arms. Sarah was in the front between her father-in-law and brother-in-law. Approximately half of the way to the hospital, Sarah heard her husband indicate that Timothy had just died. Sarah, ever the loving mom, started to be hysterical and tried to get her hands on the baby. The moments seemed like hours. Arriving at the hospital, a team of medical personnel was waiting because Sarah's mom had called and told them of the urgency. The emergency staff took the baby and rushed him in and used every possible means to resuscitate Timothy. Another doctor and other nurses attended Sarah, just cleaning up her arm and putting it into a cast temporarily not removing the bullet or bone fragments at that time.

The medical team working on Timothy was not able to revive him, so they pronounced him "dead on arrival." They found two things responsible for the baby's death. The doctor reported that, in addition to the trauma from the bullet, Timothy's head had been crushed. In the commotion, the intruder had missed the dad's head and hit the head of the baby with the butt of the gun.

Sarah's reaction to the news of Timothy's death was hysteria. She begged to be allowed to see him, thinking to herself that she could pray for God to raise him from the deathbed. She was not allowed because of concerns for her seeing the condition of the baby's head. In fact, from the moment of them taking Timothy into the emergency room, Sarah never saw her baby again. Because of the severity of wounds, the casket remained closed at the funeral.

What does one do when the initial panic begins to

wane and the realization that the event is not a nightmare but reality? Sarah said she felt betrayed, not by the intruder or the medical team, but betrayed by God. As a young Christian with no church background, she still knew that God's word teaches she had a promise. Now in those awful moments, where was the promise of protection—of help? A multitude of "what if" questions flooded her mind. What if they would have had a flat tire? What if they would have had a delay at her mom's house? Why not any kind of delay that would have changed the whole dynamic of that night?

The next part of this story is an amazing side note, which must be included to complete the picture. Seven days before Timothy was murdered, Sarah had taken her older son, Jack, to school and had Timothy in the car with her as she pulled into the driveway at their house. She heard something. Being a young Christian, she did not recognize the voice of God. As she looked over at Timothy, she related, "Something said, 'He's not going to be here very much longer.'" She thought to herself that was of the devil and so dismissed it at the time. This is an illustration of the experience of many that God does, at times, give pre-warnings of impending catastrophe. This, too, has biblical precedent. Hezekiah was warned of his own death. Joseph was warned to take Jesus and Mary to Egypt to spare Jesus' life from Herod's determination to kill Him. **We should learn from these examples that listening to the still small voice of God will much better prepare us for the difficult events of life.**

When I asked Sarah about her greatest pain in her Job

syndrome, she said that it was Timothy's absence. She struggled with missing his presence. Buying groceries or shopping for Christmas and many other day-to-day activities were full of pain because of Timothy's absence. As she continued to wrestle with the pain of missing him, Sarah still trusted God for strength on each occasion of emotional anguish. She admitted she could not bring herself to release the pain and be truly thankful to God for the changes in her life until four years had passed. Even after another son was born three years later, it was another year before she could worship God in thankfulness.

Sarah dealt with several fears like the fear of opening a closet door. She left the light on in the closet for about a year. She also made it a point to be home every day before dark, so she would not have to enter the house after dark. Her Job syndrome carried real phobias until faith was able to reach higher. At that point, in her Christian experience, Sarah admitted she did not know much about spiritual warfare. She yet continued to trust and seek God especially when at night demonic forces would wake her up and torment her. In those hours, she called on her heavenly Father, and little by little this torment was overcome.

In the process of grieving, Sarah also had to fight suicidal thoughts. She said it was like a dark room that had one white thread from top to bottom. The enemy would say, "Cut the thread and it will be all over." As with the fears, she had to pray passionately for God's help to defeat this demonic threat. She recalled that before she went into surgery to repair her arm, she asked God not to let her wake up. Relentlessly, life still demanded her attention, so she began to exhibit a real tenacity. She held on anyway. **Here is a great lesson: NEVER GIVE UP! God came through for Sarah, but He did not come instantly or even overnight. Yet, He did come!** Here, in her words, is the story of her turnaround point:

> We went to my mother's camp. One day I was lying on the bank by the lake just looking up into the sky, and I said, "Father, You could just take me; just take me now." In an instant, I saw the sky open up. I saw Jesus on a white horse, and He was coming toward me. Then, He turned to the side of me. I can still see it as if it had just happened. He leaned over just a tad and He said, "Not today, I can't take you today, and I can't come today, but I am coming soon, and I will take you then." I never asked Him to take me again. I never had those suicidal thoughts again, because I knew that He knew where I was."

Sarah's discussion went on to the question of whether she blamed God for these tragic events. She replied, "Oh, yes!...I knew He was all powerful, and I knew He could have stopped it at any moment...I knew He could have resurrected Timothy from the dead." Sarah became animated at that point. She also blamed herself. There were three different evangelists who had given prophetic words into her life that there "is healing in your hands." Her son had died. Where was the fulfillment? Why could she not help her own son? There was also a guilt because she never had the opportunity to lay her hands on Timothy to pray for him. She questioned, "Why do I need healing in my hands, when I can't heal my own child?" It is amazing how often people who are called by God and purposed for a specific ministry will experience events (sometimes catastrophic) that go contrary or in an opposite direction to the ministry itself.

I asked Sarah if, after all the years, she has discovered an answer to the question, "Why did this happen to me?" I think her answer is profound. She said, "Yes and no." She explained that by saying, "Ever since I accepted Jesus, the Holy Ghost has dropped something down in me...I knew I had a purpose...This happened to further my purpose." Although Sarah could not understand or explain why this played out in her life the way it did, she is absolutely convinced that it was and is a part of God's purpose for her.

At the beginning of her Christian experience, Sarah had said to God, "Do with me what You will!" In her naiveté about Christian things and the Bible, she did not realize that Mary, the mother of Jesus, had made a similar surrender to God's purpose in her life when she said, "Behold the handmaid of the Lord; be it unto me according to thy word." (Luke 1:38) Sarah could not see, nor could she have known in any real sense, how her surrender to God would be challenged by such trying events during the years to come.

Here is another lesson in God's ways. We tend to

see our lives in a series of individual events like links in a chain. We concentrate on one link at a time. We cannot see the whole chain, because many of the links of our lives are not yet formed. Incredibly, God sees the whole chain at once. He is the Designer and Constructor Who adds each link in the exact place it needs to be. The problem with this simile of links in a chain is that most chains have links, which are uniform in size, shape and weight, while the links of our lives are an infinite variety of sizes, shapes, and weights. Occasionally, one of the large links in our lives is a Job syndrome.

As I continued the interview with Sarah about the question, "Why," she was moved with a preacher's anointing. She talked of her new discovery of God. In humility and great, animated wonder, she said, "It was all about me seeing God for Who He is in His glory, power and majesty. That He is God! And, He didn't owe me anything, but I owed Him everything."

I then asked if she had developed a message from her Job syndrome. She quickly said, "The three things He spoke to me back then are the three things I still tell people today who are in distress: first, 'I, God, am more than enough;' second, 'My grace is sufficient;' and, third, 'I am made strong in your weakness…so, if you are never weak, how can I show up strong?'" Sarah continued, "None of us want to be in a weak place where we can't get ourselves out of a fix, but that is the circumstance where God's strength is greatest in our lives."

Finally, I asked whether there was an overarching

lesson from her Job syndrome experience. She related this story, "One time in worship, it was…like a cloud had settled on me, and in that moment, nothing else mattered but God…I said this with my mouth, 'Thank You! I have buried a child, and I know that You are more than enough for my life…thank You for allowing me to experience You in that way!'" That is a truly astounding result of such a trial. Many people and even some readers might not be able to fully comprehend the import of such an experience with our Heavenly Father, but it was totally real to Sarah

Sarah has gone on to serve the Lord for many years since her Job syndrome. She has become an ordained minister, and more recently, a fulltime missionary to Cameroon, Africa. Her four-year appointment was cut short due to the ongoing danger from rebel bombings near her area of labor. Since coming home to the United States of America, she has been diagnosed with stage four colon cancer and has gone through another Job syndrome challenging her faith and her destiny. Knowing the righteous and godly nature of Sarah, one of Father's chosen daughters, I, along with others, was believing with her that a healing deliverance was working for her good. Our Father had already begun the work. Two weeks after the original diagnosis and with much prayer going up for her, she was re-evaluated at stage two. Miraculously, she is now cancer free and continuing to minister through God's mercy and grace. Sarah's experience illustrates many of the symptoms of a Job syndrome, as we will see now in more detail.

Job's Example

The basis of the Job syndrome and the book itself is Job's righteous life. Had Job been a sinner, by one sin or many, there would be no example; there would be no book. He would have been just another believer who failed and received his just punishment, hardly anything new to demand space in the canon of scripture. Good intentioned people still join themselves to Job's comforters and accuse him of sin such as: (1) he had pride in his innocence; (2) he blasphemed God in his accusations, and (3) he brought everything on himself through the sin of fear. Each of these accusations deserves at least a quick rebuttal, since no one in the Job syndrome needs to hear those same accusations.

First, as to the accusation of pride, Job had confidence in his innocence; not once did he speak of it in a boastful spirit. Job saw his innocence as his life of faithfulness to God in morality and in worship. He also knew he had functioned in dedicated commitment as a priest for his family. We should note, since God was against the pride in Leviathan (Job 41:34), He certainly would have brought that up with Job if he were sinning the sin of pride.

Second, as to the accusation of blasphemy, when God spoke of Job in chapter 42, He said that Job had spoken "rightly" of Him, and He called him "my servant" (42:8). If Job's complaints to God had been truly offensive to Him, then surely, He would have called that to Job's attention just as He corrected Eliphaz and the other two friends. Job confessed for talking about the things of God with an inadequate knowledge as though he understood those things (Job 42:3-6). Yet, God never held him responsible for saying the so-called "sinful" things about Him. Blasphemy is a serious charge in the teachings of the Scripture. Nowhere in the Bible is that charge leveled against Job.

Third, as to the accusation of the sin of fear, the verse so often used to say Job brought on his own troubles through fear is 3:25 where Job said, "For the thing I greatly feared is come upon me." The false teaching on this verse is based on an interpretation of "the thing" as the calamity, which Job suffered. In view of what the book of Job actually tells us, this cannot be the correct interpretation. The author said once, and God said twice, that Job had fear (Job 1:1, 8; 2:3). JOB'S FEAR WAS OF GOD! This holy awe for God was an extreme motivation in Job's life to worship. He respected God and His judgment with a healthy reverential fear. Job interpreted his several calamities to be a judgment from God, but his great perplexity was that he could not discern why for he was innocent. Also, there are good arguments from the grammar that his fear did not cause his problems. Job's statement is in the singular, which relates to what Job perceived to be God's punishment rather than to his own tragedies. He did not say, "The things I greatly feared..." Finally, the repetitious second statement in the second stich of the verse is from the parallelism of the Hebrew poetry and not from an additional fear.

I admit that **these last three arguments have come**

to be a major concern to me in the light of some teaching which refuses to accept the reality of "innocent" people going through suffering. The essence of such teaching is to make the sufferer the cause of his or her own suffering. I believe this result is unintended in most cases, but, nevertheless, it effectively heaps a guilt trip on the sufferer since he must have sinned or is plagued with a lack of faith to be delivered from his or her personal calamity. This, again, was the accusation of Job's friends, which proved to be invalid in Job's case. The modern church should be finding ways to encourage the Christian sufferers rather than accusing them of sin, lack of spirituality, or lack of faith. The examples of many in the Bible and the examples illustrated in this book show innocent, good, and faith-filled people living in reverential fear of God, yet they are attacked by that wicked *Satan*.

Job's example as a person living by faith and obedience to the commands of God certainly went far beyond normalcy. **Job was literally, God's bragging point.** God had said that no one on earth could match Job as a man of devotion and right living (Job 1:8; 2:3). Job walked with God in a most unique way reverencing Him as *El Shaddai*, the Almighty, and he exemplified the highest degree of piety and devotion. He was the man to whom others looked for help (Job 29:7-16). Job was a righteous man, and that meant he was constantly being benevolent and offering his wise counsel, whenever he was called upon to give it. Yet, evil (in the sense of tragedy and affliction) came to him, and he endured the attack while responding rightly to it. That is an example to follow. We will now look at ways to prepare to be more like Job in patient endurance and faith.

Dealing with Self in the Process

We are too often challenged with boredom. Life gets in a rut of the everyday, everyday, everyday—the same old, the same old and the same old! Well, you get the point. What do we do with a Christian experience that offers nothing really new? How do we react when corporate worship seems dull and unexciting; when prayer seems to bounce off the ceiling; when Bible reading puts you to sleep; when paying a tithe and giving only drains the bank account? **In other words, how do we deal with our faith when, seemingly, there are no benefits?** The Psalmist was at a similar place when he wrote in Psalm 73:2-3, "But as for me, my feet were almost gone; my steps had well nigh slipped. For I was envious at the foolish, when I saw the prosperity of the wicked." When even the wicked are doing well and being prosperous, we seem to fall into the despair of Job. Why try?

The problem at this point is not God or His plan. The problem here is self-centeredness. All of the above questions are in fact very conceited. Is our Christianity all about us, or is it all about Father? **When we are concerned about what is in it for us, we miss the call of our loving Father to abide in His bosom and to commune with His heart. We cannot love our Father**

God properly and to the right proportion when we are consumed with self.

A part of Job's difficulties was his self-concern, but he did not press it to the point of idolatry. When we are too much troubled with our "children," our "things" and our "boils," we too will complain and question. We will probably not be as eloquent as Job, but certainly as mouthy. This proclivity to self-absorption is a major impediment to faith. **Faith cannot live long in the environment of self-importance or its cousins: vanity, narcissism, conceit, selfishness and egotism. To the measure we allow elements of any of these idolatrous characteristics in our lives, we will be subtracting a proportional measure from true faith in God.**

An argument can be made that a certain self-awareness is necessary, and that it is good. Did not Jesus say, "Love your neighbor AS YOURSELF?" (Matthew 22:39 NIV, emphasis mine) Jesus knew that He had created in us enough love of self to strongly motivate us to self-preservation both physically and spiritually. Of course, we cannot go through life without some self-awareness. Yet, we must remember that Biblical self-awareness is rooted and grounded in humility. The following passages clearly illustrate the necessity of humility.

> Whosoever therefore shall humble himself as this little child, the same is greatest in the kingdom of heaven.
>
> -Matthew 18:4

But he giveth more grace. Wherefore he saith, God resisteth the proud, but giveth grace unto the humble.

-James 4:6

Likewise, ye younger, submit yourselves unto the elder. Yea, all of you be subject one to another, and be clothed with humility: for God resisteth the proud, and giveth grace to the humble. Humble yourselves therefore under the mighty hand of God, that he may exalt you in due time.

-1 Peter 5:5-6

We can observe in the lives of biblical characters and in our own lives a degeneration from total submission in humility to God to utter rebellion against Him in pride, or worse, a covering of our religious pride with a façade of spiritual superiority. It was this religious hypocrisy in the Pharisees and Sadducees, which Jesus attacked so vehemently in Matthew 23.

At the point of our salvation, there was an all-inclusive yielding. There was not one reservation or accommodation of self. We gave Him our all. From that wonderful beginning, far too often there are steps of regression, which lessen our submission and yielding to Father. Our adversary, *the Satan*, has constantly plagued us with temptations of self-absorption. For an example, have you ever been tempted with pride, which thinks, "My belief system and brand of Christianity is better than theirs," or "I know I am living more righteously than most Christians?" You see, it really is a matter of the attitude of the heart.

Christian maturity can be summed up in this: it is coming to yield all of one's self, with no reservation, at all times, that Jesus Christ may be all in all. When any element of self is present, that Christian is in need of another repenting, another "dunk," another cleansing. That does not mean getting "saved" again, but it is the process of sanctification which the old-timers had right, especially the Wesleyans. When one can truly say, "Less of me and more of God," there is a wonderful freedom, which comes with such abandonment. Romans 6, 7, and 8 is a life-changing study on the process of sanctification taking us from self to God, from "flesh" to "Spirit." A very honest humility is the result when we learn that "our old man is crucified with [H]im." (Romans 6:6)

When Job repented in sackcloth and ashes, he exemplified the kind of humility and consecration that we are discussing. **There is no substitute. There is no alternative. Self-centeredness must go. The humility that comes from a real encounter with God must overtake, overwhelm and consume our lives.**

MY PRAYER

My Father, I am pricked in my heart. I keep trying to beat down the self in me that is so ugly and repugnant to me and abhorrent to You. I have tried to crucify myself over and over. I cannot succeed. Help me to see and know that I died in the death of my Lord Jesus. "I am crucified with Christ." Forgive my pride, my bragging and my self-absorption. Once again, I yield!

7
DIVINING THE TRUTH ABOUT THE GOD OF JOB

Surely no one lays a hand on a broken man
    when he cries for help in his distress.
Have I not wept for those in trouble?
    Has not my soul grieved for the poor?
Yet when I hoped for good, evil came;
    when I looked for light, then came darkness.
The churning inside me never stops;
    days of suffering confront me.
I go about blackened, but not by the sun;
    I stand up in the assembly and cry for help.
I have become a brother of jackals,
    a companion of owls.
My skin grows black and peels;
    my body burns with fever.
My harp is tuned to mourning,
    and my flute to the sound of wailing.
                    -Job 30:24-31 (NIV)

I knew most of her story, because I had experienced a lot of it with her and the family. She was and is a great and faithful friend, and her name is Linda. When I interviewed her for this testimony, I really did not expect this for an opening. She said, "I'm awfully glad that time has passed, and I can be able to talk about this...probably, in the beginning after mom passed, my view of things would have been different, but now, after prayer and God working in my life, I see a lot more."[66]

Linda's story of her Job syndrome began with the death of her husband in 2002. It is interesting that our interview was on the anniversary of the date. The following summer she took her mother to the wedding of Linda's son. It was at that time Linda discovered her mother had a serious problem. She knew that it was going to be difficult for her. Because of family situations, she anticipated she would have to be the caregiver, so at the time, she did not say anything to anyone. Linda's mother was in the early stage of the development of Alzheimer's disease. At that point, it was only Linda "that she showed herself to." Esther, Linda's mother, was staying with her during that summer. After a few weeks, her mother cried with sadness and longing as she wanted to go home during the month of August, which she did. Linda's trials were only beginning. By January, she had moved to Florida from her home in Connecticut, taking Esther with her. She had suffered her third loss by having to sell her house to which she was very attached. This house was always the center of family activities, especially the holidays.

Three traumas within just over a year began to bring a buildup of emotional pain, and the questions began. Linda recalled, "I had been praying and asking the Lord what He wanted." Just before he passed, on his deathbed, her husband had come to know the Lord as his Savior. During that time, Linda remembered getting down one night alone and praying, "Everything is just whirling around; what do You want?" She realized she was at the end of herself and couldn't do anything, so she prayed, "Above all else, I want Your will whether I like it or not—show me what to do." That can be a dangerous prayer but the right prayer. Her children began insisting on her selling the house. She told them if they wanted it sold, they would have to sell it. Three days later a young couple bought the house. They wanted to be in the house before Thanksgiving, and that was three weeks away. Linda said that she began a "protestation" to God. He reminded her, "You said, 'I want Your will.'" She added, "So, I shut up." Incredibly, by January, Linda was moved to Florida with her mother. She said, "I went with the thought, 'I'm glad to take care of my mother, but I'll be home soon.'"

The development of the disease was a slow process. Linda knew her mother had Alzheimer's disease, but she was not sharing that with anyone yet. The real journey began from there. Linda said, "I was the one she fought right from the beginning." Her mother's prayer had always been that she didn't want to live with her children, and she didn't want to lose her mind. Linda recalled being frustrated with the fact that the prayer of her mother was not answered. This was her question, "Lord, she's been faithful; she's worked for You all these years, and You didn't answer her." Through the ordeal, Linda discovered that the journey was her own. It was Linda's trial of faith.

Her mother, Esther, was unaware of a problem.

Early in the trial, God sent her a friend, Abby, to help her "walk this journey out." During the summer of that year, there were four hurricanes. Through many days of wind and rain with time consumed mostly indoors, Linda and Abby spent much of that time together, and in Linda's words, they "had a ball." As with Job, it is truly amazing how God puts people in our lives to help shape the outcome of a Job syndrome. In a short period of time, God gave Linda another friend and prayer partner. That lady was none other than my sister, Alethea, a strong woman of prayer who has journeyed through her own Job syndrome by suffering a traumatic divorce and the consequent move cross country with two teenage children. These three ladies fought many spiritual battles in the course of Linda's Job syndrome.

The tension between Linda and Esther slowly began to worsen. Still, Esther was able to appear normal to others. These were very difficult times. Linda said, "My mother in the Alzheimer's was so stubborn and so miserable…It's hard to talk about my mother in that way…To everyone around her she was sweet, and she was sweet—she was a sweet woman." Linda continued, "She had lived for God for years…Due to her, each one of her children came to the Lord…It was because of her faithfulness that my dad gave his life to the Lord after forty years." Among her other accomplishments as a Christian, Esther was a group leader in her church. She was the treasurer, took care of the books and became the missionary leader. Linda put it this way, "She did everything they asked her to do—she was faithful." Her house was full most of the time as she entertained guest ministers, even overseers and missionaries. "She was a wonderful, wonderful woman," Linda added emotionally.

Now things were all different as Linda was dealing with this person who treated her hatefully. She recalled that she took that treatment personally. She said, "It took me four years to come to the conclusion that I had to stop being hurt by the personal stuff, because it wasn't her any longer." The other stressor Linda suffered was when she realized she would not be moving back to Connecticut where the rest of her family lived.

Linda spoke of the "one saving grace," which was discovering a new church home where the pastor (my brother, Troy) was a great preacher and teacher of the Word. This church had an extremely blessed music program in which she got involved. Church activities and new church friends, including my wife and me as associate pastors, became a welcome and needed distraction from the emotional pressure at home. At that time, there was room in the schedule for Linda to participate, since her mother had not progressed to the point of needing 24-hour care.

Linda continued the description of her mom, Esther, "Mom became more and more…violent is the word I'm going to use…She was completely different." Esther's violent side was only toward her caregiver, her daughter, Linda. It was a very painful time for her. She was beginning to experience the full effect of her own Job syndrome.

Linda observed, "This Alzheimer's thing is a horrible thing...It's an awful thing to watch someone go through, but it's worse watching someone taking care of them go through it." She added, "Losing one's mind makes everything so difficult."

At that point, Linda summed up one of the lessons she learned, **"There is a significant difference in the physical man and the spiritual man." The spiritual man is intact**. She said, "The physical man can go, and the mind can go; but the spirit is there, and the Holy Ghost is there." Her mother would be miserable and swearing at Linda saying terrible things, but she would walk into church, raise her hands and her spirit-man would take over. As she praised God and worshiped, the tears would flow. She would hug other people and love on them with a genuine passion. In what was becoming a very burdensome trial for Linda, God was teaching her wonderful lessons of relationship, love, and trust through the process. Here is one of the memories she related:

> Because I was holding so much in, I didn't realize how emotional I was under the stress. Walking outside of church one night and talking to one of the girls, all these things inside began to come out. The more I talked, the angrier I became. I didn't want to be there. It wasn't my choice. Why was God doing this to me? Why did my mother hate me?
>
> Before the process of all this, my mom and I had a wonderful experience together. We had a great

relationship all our lives. It was a spiritual relationship as well as a mother and daughter…All of a sudden, we are in this situation: "My mother hated my guts," I thought…Why did God do this to me? Why did the Lord bring me here, so my mother doesn't like me and just to have me feel this way after all these years? Why did it have to be me?

I remember it was Abby as she stood there with tears running down her face. She had been quiet, and Abby is not a quiet person. She finally said, "It's because you needed to take care of your mother…she needed you, not anybody else." I didn't know what to say to that.

As that journey continued and progressed into the Alzheimer's disease, the more I knew I wanted to serve the Lord. I saw God in her, and I saw what He did for her. I saw what He did for me. That was the hardest journey of my whole life, but it was the most rewarding at the end of it.

Linda's testimony covered many other details of the trying nature of the situation with her mother and, also, some of the many "small" miracles of God's grace and provision. In Linda's Job syndrome, it took on a little different nature, once again demonstrating the individuality of a Job syndrome. **There wasn't just one God moment. There were many times Father made Himself real by enabling her to deal with the latest surprise difficulty of the progression of the disease in her mother.** I will share two of the most significant times.

The first is a period of time Esther was having nightmares. They were really bad nightmares. As she experienced the horrible nightmares, Linda recalled:

> She was screaming and talking. I could hear sounds. I thought she was praying, but she wasn't. She was talking in the mirror and remembering her life before she knew Christ. The enemy was bringing up her past. She was talking in the mirror to herself, and I knew it wasn't of God. I didn't understand, and I questioned what's going on here. One night I heard the screaming, and I ran to her bedroom almost severely injuring myself. She was standing, holding her head, and screaming, "I can't go through this anymore; I can't do this anymore!"
>
> I sat her down, took her in my arms and prayed for her, "Lord, you have to do something; You can't let her go through torment this way; This is not of You." It was a very difficult night. The next day I had someone to stay with mom, so I came to church. Pastor Lemuel was there. I did not know what else to do, so I said to him, "Somebody has to pray for my mother..." I then told him about the nightmares and the trauma. He took it to heart. He got up, stopped the service and said, "Linda needs us to pray for Esther...she is having dreams...I'm having dreams...Is anybody having dreams?" A bunch of people came forward, and he asked me to stand in for my mother. He began to pray for the minds of people, and he prayed for different ones. I knew that God was going to do something. From that moment, my mother never had another nightmare. She never looked in the mirror and talked to herself again. That oppressive spirit was gone.

Once again, the dynamics of a Job syndrome showed that **faithfulness to God in times of struggle brings a response from Him. It is also very clear that God's response is always "tailor made" to each individual syndrome. The principle is that He does respond! The experience is that the timing, method, or result of the response cannot be predicted. It will be for our best on an eternal scale.**

The second God encounter, which Linda had, came in another extreme struggle, again over a period of time. It had to do with a spirit of death. Esther was refusing to eat and getting weaker and weaker. There were people who were coming to Linda's house quite regularly. Even then, a lot of prayer was going up while Esther was progressively getting frail. Listen to the story in Linda's own words:

> Mom started going downhill. She was sick and very tired. My brother, Rex was coming down from Connecticut a lot. Every time he came down, there was a reason. We would pray through another crisis. We had lots of prayer. He was down on this particular day. An English immigrant friend, Moe, was there. I remember Rex was sitting on the couch, and I knew something was wrong. I didn't know what…He couldn't concentrate. Rex stood up and started to go toward my mother's bedroom. She was lying in bed. I got up and began to walk the hallway. Abby got up and walked to the door of my bedroom. We just walked and prayed. Rex closed the door to mom's bedroom and was praying. I remember him getting wilder as he prayed. After a

while, he came back into the living room and sat down again. I knew something was not right. He wasn't paying attention, and finally he said, "It's not done yet."

Rex got up and walked back into the bedroom closing the door behind him…He looked at my mother and said, "You foul spirit of death be gone in the name of Jesus." Before he did that, he placed his daughter in one spot in the house. He placed Abby in front of my bedroom door; he put me in the kitchen, and we all began to pray. As we prayed, I started jumping like a jumping Jack. I started praising. I could only praise. All of a sudden when I heard him say that, the Holy Spirit hit that house. A breeze went through the house. We slammed open the door of her bedroom…The next morning my mother got up and started eating and asking for coffee. From that moment on things were changed.

As Linda recalled that event, she noticeably enthused over the wonderful victory of that God-moment when He broke off the spirit of death over her mother. It was a great victory for each one who participated in the deliverance prayer. As Linda described it, "It was one of those times that God switched things around, and He changed them so tangibly that you couldn't deny it."

Ten years of the progressively worsening disease in Linda's mother, Esther, took a toll on Linda emotionally. She approached a total breakdown on more than one occasion. Symptoms like uncontrollable crying, hopelessness, and fits of screaming at God brought her to the brink of emotional disaster. Yet, God in His mercy sustained her, even miraculously restoring her on one extreme occasion.

There is a Job syndrome-like ending to Linda's story. Here is her recollection:

> That was the hardest journey of my whole life, but it was also the most rewarding at the end of it. The disease took my mother down to almost nothing. Though she had to go through the mental thing, and though the physical destroyed her (the Alzheimer's took her right down to the bone), she loved God 'til she took her last breath. At the end of this, she would raise her hands and praise God in motions when she couldn't even talk. Her children would sing and join in the praise. The last…three weeks when she had stopped eating, I saw the love of God become so strong, and she became so sweet in the Spirit. She herself did not suffer. People around her suffered, but she didn't. It was an easy passing for her.
>
> Everything had changed. I knew that it was my thing. I knew that I had to be with her. I had to protect her in the hospital and later in a facility for professional end-time care. I would look at her and say, "Mom, please eat." She would look back at me with such sorrowful yet knowing eyes and say, "No," then touch my hand lovingly.
>
> While she was in the hospital just before the end, there was a beautiful experience I had with her. I looked over at her, and she wasn't there anymore. She was looking around the room and smiling. She was nodding her head and pointing at people. I could tell it was people as she continued to nod and smile. She then said, "Soon!" She had no idea I was

there. I knew that I knew that all was well, and God had blessed me.

Linda's description of Esther's last three weeks was a portrayal of a scene in total peace and victory. As her Associate Pastor, I was there experiencing that peace along with Linda, her family, and the other prayer warriors who had been along for much of the fight against the disease of Alzheimer's and its effects. For ten years, Linda stood faithful in defiance of the multi-pronged attacks of *the Satan*. Actually, Linda's story is one of triumph! Yes, most of the ten years were filled with struggle and, at times, deep loneliness, but the God-moments, as in other Job syndromes, miraculously and supernaturally sustained Linda and incrementally changed the dynamics of her faith and trust in God. **One should never underestimate the value of the personal changes made while enduring a Job syndrome.** It is this constantly changing dynamic of a Job syndrome that we now approach in a theological way. I hope to offer a better understanding of the character and ways of our God Who occasionally allows a Job syndrome in the lives of some of His most faithful people.

Perceiving the God of Job

One of the major concepts of the God of Job is GOD'S RELATIONSHIP TO EVIL. Job was smitten with evil by *the Satan* who had his permission and authority from God. **"Evil" is one of the keywords of the Job syndrome along with affliction, faith, witness,**

innocence, and others. William C. Williams made an astute comment, "As a prerequisite for any discussion of evil, moral evil must be distinguished from physical or natural evil."[67] He also added that the Bible never attributes moral evil to God; in fact, He hates this kind of evil.[68] An example is in Psalm 5:4-6:

> For thou art not a God that hath pleasure in wickedness: neither shall evil dwell with thee. The foolish shall not stand in thy sight: thou hatest all workers of iniquity. Thou shalt destroy them that speak leasing: the Lord will abhor the bloody and deceitful man.

On the other hand, God claims to be the creator of evil (physical or natural) as in Isaiah 45:7, "I form the light, and create darkness: I make peace, and create evil: I the Lord do all these things." And, once again, in Job, the evil that came to him is said to be from God:

> But he said unto her, Thou speakest as one of the foolish women speaketh. What? shall we receive good at the hand of God, and shall we not receive evil? In all this did not Job sin with his lips.
> -Job 2:10

> God hath delivered me to the ungodly, and turned me over into the hands of the wicked. I was at ease, but he hath broken me asunder: he hath also taken me by my neck, and shaken me to pieces, and set me up for his mark. His archers compass me round

about, he cleaveth my reins asunder, and doth not spare; he poureth out my gall upon the ground. He breaketh me with breach upon breach, he runneth upon me like a giant.

-Job 16:11-14

For destruction from God was a terror to me, and by reason of his highness I could not endure.

-Job 31:23

As I discussed previously, **God is ultimately responsible for the calamities Job experienced. God never refuted His culpability in Job's trial, yet He also bore full responsibility for putting limitations on the extent of the trial.** In the first wave of calamity, *Satan* was told by God, "…Behold, all that he hath is in thy power; only upon himself put not forth thine hand. So *Satan* went forth from the presence of the Lord." (Job 1:12) In the second wave of evil against Job, God told *the Satan* that he must save Job's life, "…Behold, he is in thine hand; but save his life." (Job 2:6)

God's limitation boundaries are on every trial allowed! Hallelujah! What an encouragement! Here is **another key lesson from Job: GOD IS IN CONTROL** even when it seems He has forgotten or is ignoring our extreme suffering. Satan does not have full authority. He is limited in every case on an individual basis. We must **KNOW** when in deepest despair that our loving Father has placed limitations on our attacker. The apostle Paul put it this way in 1 Corinthians 10:13, "No temptation has overtaken you but such as is common to man; and God is faithful, who will not allow you to be tempted beyond what you are able, but with the temptation will provide the way of escape also, so that you will be able to endure it." (NASB) **The fact of God's control over your Job syndrome should be a major source of hope and comfort. Take heart! He has not abandoned you.** Listen to what the Holy Spirit says to us through the apostle James, "Blessed is the man who perseveres under trial, because when he has stood the test, he will receive the crown of life that God has promised to those who love him." (James 1:12, NIV)

Another major concept about God with which to be reckoned in Job is the MYSTERY OF GOD. Job found it very difficult to deal with God's unpredictability. His tragedies came as a total surprise. According to Job's concepts of God's expected behavior (retributive justice), God should still be blessing him with health and prosperity, because he had been faithful in obedient righteous living. **What does a person do when life takes hard turns and God is unpredictable—He does not do as He has promised?** God did not, in any way, owe Job anything. Their relationship before, during, and after the trial was not based on juridical obligation, but on God's loving grace and Job's free, open, and trusting (no matter what) response. The message of the gospel fifteen hundred years before it was preached and two thousand years since it began to be preached is that **GOD GAVE,** not that He owed. He gave Job his blessings before the trial. He gave Job double blessings after the trial, and He even gave the trial. He still freely gives.

Here is an important question: "If God is a covenant-keeping God, how do we reconcile that with the God of mystery?" The word *covenant* appears twice in Job, and neither time does it refer to God, but the idea of covenant lies behind much of the argument on retribution. There should be no doubt that God is a covenant-keeping God. However, several comments seem appropriate. First, **God's covenants are authored by God, which means they are not authored, nor even co-authored, by man in his limited language and governed by man-centered concepts. Since God is the author of His covenants, it must be understood that the terms of His covenants are defined in His omniscience and eternity, not by human understandings or the words men use. The covenants and promises of scripture, written in the language of men, are God's condescended way of expressing Himself so that a part of His much greater cause and purpose may be known and followed.** God's understanding of His terms goes far beyond "answer," "heal," "provide," "deliver," or "now." God refuses to be limited by man's ideas or language. He is not bound in any way to explain Himself, since the chasm between understandings is too deep. He is certainly capable of explaining Himself, but man is incapable of grasping the unlimited nature of His ways. **Believers of every age have found it necessary to add their faith to their** understanding of His applicable promise and to wait expectantly for the fulfillment, which proceeds from His word, within His understanding of the terms, which is based in His holiness, omniscience, eternality, and grace.** The saying of St. Paul "...we see through a glass, darkly," (1 Corinthians 13:12) is never more truthfully realized than when one is going through a Job syndrome. **Faith will walk you through the dark places! No matter what is happening in my life or yours, we must trust God's wisdom in bringing us into the glory of sonship with Him.**

Another aspect of the God of Job, which is not obvious in the text, is **GOD'S ULTIMATE PURPOSE. God's bottom line is the salvation of souls.** The theme of salvation-history, or the thread of redemption, runs through the entire Bible, and it does not bypass Job. Job acted as priest for his family and interceded for his friends offering atoning sacrifices. Job continued the truth that "without shedding of blood is no remission." (Hebrews 9:22) The apostle Peter said that God's will was for "all to come to repentance" (2 Peter 2:9). The Hebrews writer said that Jesus' death, resurrection, and exaltation was the God-like thing to do "in bringing many sons unto glory" (Heb. 2:10). The apostle Paul, in Ephesians, taught God's ultimate purpose in choosing "us in [H]im before the foundation of the world," was for His intention of adopting His children (making us as believers His family) and gathering together all things in Christ (Eph. 1:5, 10).

It follows then, that God's dealing with people is

always working toward the salvation of the individual and the salvation of all others who fall under the influence of that person. This was the case with Job relative to his family, his friends, and most probably to his servants as well as a host of peripheral acquaintances (42:10-11). So, it will be also with any person going through the Job syndrome. **God uses believers, and sometimes, suffering believers, as examples to get to others.** Such truth does not ease the immediate suffering, but it does offer a goal, which should highly motivate endurance.

In anticipation of possible rebuttals centered in the passage in James that says, "For God cannot be tempted by evil, nor does he tempt anyone" (James 1:13a, NIV), the following exegesis is offered. First, there are two reasons for the impossibility of tempting God. God cannot be tempted in the sense of being tried and tested for He is both perfect and omnipotent. What thought or thing could touch that? Nor can God be tempted in the sense of thinking or doing moral wrong or sin, because He is radically holy! But, men are not God, and they do not have His attributes. People are subject to temptation, therefore the Job syndrome. It has been the position in this writing that God was ultimately responsible for Job's trial, so how does that not conflict with James' statement that God is not responsible for temptation?

James himself gives the answer, "[E]ach one is tempted when, by his own evil desire he is dragged away and enticed" (James 1:14, NIV). The "evil desire" in this passage is from the Greek word *epithumia*, which means a strong, controlling, or obsessive desire.[69] This word is one of my favorite words in the New Testament since an understanding of it explains so much. It can mean a positive (good) desire or a negative (evil) desire. But, either way, it does have the meaning of an obsessive desire. A person then is only tempted from within in the process of deciding upon a response to a potentially sinful stimulus. The stimulus, which God places, or allows *the Satan* to place, in the life of the person is not in or of itself the sin or even the temptation. The temptation, according to James (and he must be right), is from within, or in Joban language, from Behemoth, the untamable beast within. We do not want to hear that, for we all have the inclination to blame some thing or someone for our own failures. There must be an admission on our part that there is a beast within controlled by evil desire (*epithumia*). God may allow the stimulus, but we are tempted or tried by our own inner struggle. The antidote for the failures of the flesh is given in a fantastic revelation in the writings of Paul. In his letter to the Galatians (5:16), he wrote, "This I say then, Walk in the Spirit, and ye shall not fulfil the lust of the flesh." The word "lust" here is from that Greek word again, *epithumia*. Walking in the Spirit every moment will prevent the diversions and obsessions of wrong thoughts and desires.

Modern Ministry to the Job Syndrome

I would like to propose several concepts related to encouraging people who are going through a Job syndrome. To approach ministry to those in the Job syndrome will necessitate an understanding of the dynamics of Job's trial, his response, and his recovery. **There must be an awareness of the Job syndrome being much larger than the person experiencing it.** It is obvious that if a person experiencing tragedy, affliction, or emotional pain could change it, they would. **There is a cosmic or supernatural dimension to suffering.** Whether in the life of a believer or unbeliever, the design of *the Satan* is to cause one to curse, or at the least, to disavow God or His will in the matter. **God's purpose in allowing the suffering may be disciplinary, didactic, prophetic (in the sense of warning), or "for nothing"** (Job 2:3 translated by Wolfers).[70] Without pushing too close to dualism, the Job syndrome in the lives of people is the direct result of *the Satan's* conflict with God. Lacocque had wonderful insights on this point showing that believers are involved with God in engaging the conflict against evil and this is a proof of man's free will. Lacocque stated, "In short, the very opposition or conflict between good and evil in the universe is a guarantee that the divine-human relationship is characterized by freedom (versus manipulation) and love...."[71]

Hebrews 11 teaches that all real accomplishment in the Kingdom of God is wrought by and through faith. **As much as the Job syndrome is an exercise in endurance, there could be no endurance without faith laying hold of the substance of hopeful anticipation, and its grasping the unseen evidence (Heb. 11:1). For the believer, the Job syndrome is a journey, more**

appropriately, a pilgrimage of faith. Job, even while in the bitterness of his complaint, moved from faith to faith. In his commentary of Job 19:25, Robert Gordis described Job as having discovered new faith "forged in the crucible of his undeserved suffering."[72] The progression of Job's faith was explained so beautifully by Gordis that an extended quotation is germane. In his discussion of Job's famous statement, "I know that my Redeemer lives," Gordis said:

> Now Job undergoes a complete transformation of mood, the most striking in the book, although not the only one. This sudden and drastic change of temper, which leaves the logician helpless, is entirely credible psychologically. From the depths of despair, Job soars to the height of faith. Twice before he has stood poised on the brink—ready to deny life and its Giver—but each time he recoiled from the abyss and found his way to a stronger affirmation of life's meaning. In his torrential outpouring of speech, we find not a systematic development of thought but an upward-sweeping spiral of feeling. Job's soul is an ocean, surging with the flow and ebb of the tide—each wave of faith rushes in on the strand and then falls back under the impact of his loneliness and pain. Then a new and more powerful breaker roars in further upon the shore, until it too recedes with the tide. In his first round, Job expresses a longing for an arbiter (*mōkkiaḥ*) who might judge between him and his Adversary (9: 32-33). In the second outpouring of faith, Job's wish becomes a firm conviction that there already stands a witness (*sēdh*)

in the heavens ready to testify on his behalf (16:19). Now Job reaches the peak of his faith. In a moment of mystical ecstasy, he sees his vindication: a redeemer who will not merely speak but will act to avenge his suffering (19:25). The term he uses, *goel*, means a kinsman, a blood-avenger, who in early Hebrew law was duty-bound to see that justice was done to his injured brother.[73]

Job's faith was not built on the Word of God, for none of the Holy Bible had been written as yet. Job's faith was built on the oral tradition passed down from Adam and Seth. This was a tradition, which the Pentateuch written by Moses later revealed and explained. You see, God's revelation has always been available to those who desired to know about Him. **Today we are without excuse for not knowing Father's way and will as relates to salvation, since it is clearly documented in the Scripture.** We too can have the "upward-sweeping spiral" of faith that Job had if we only trust the revealed truth about God.

True biblical faith, for us, must be based on a working understanding of God's word as the Apostle Paul wrote, "So then faith cometh by hearing, and hearing by the word of God." (Rom. 10:17) **Faith in its basic meaning is a reliance on the word, power, love and ultimate justice of *Yahweh*, the God of relationship.** Faith is man's side of the relationship. Responding to that faith within His all-knowing and His all-loving is in fact God's great delight and pleasure. How thrilled (if that is not a too-human term) was *Yahweh* to give back to Job double of everything, not out of obligation, but out of grace!

There can be no endurance of the Job syndrome without hope that, at some point on one's personal timeline, circumstances will change for the better. Job exhibited very typical human emotions from near total despair to great pinnacles of hope and faith as discussed by Gordis above. One of the times of hope came out of an insight Job had on what was happening to him. He confessed it beautifully, "But he knows the way that I take; / when he has tested me, I shall come forth as gold" (23:10, Hartley).[74] The verse written by Peter that has been so challenging to me personally seems to be a paraphrase of Job's statement. Peter wrote, "That the trial of your faith, being much more precious than of gold that perisheth, though it be tried with fire, might be found unto praise and honor and glory at the appearing of Jesus Christ" (1 Pet. 1:7). **The phrase "trial of your faith" speaks the essence of the Job syndrome.** Job's hope and confidence expected a good outcome, "as gold." The person in the Job syndrome needs to remember and to continue the metaphor. **As gold is valued by its purity, so also is faith.** Impurities, whether from gold in its natural state or from intentional alloy, must be removed by applying the heat from fire. **According to Peter and Job, trial functions, like the fire, to purify faith. To push the metaphor beyond the scripture (but, hopefully still in the spirit of the scripture), does the sufferer desire 10-, 14-, 18-, 22-, or 24-karat faith?** The proof is in the Job-like trial of fire. Once again, **it is all about the goal, not the experience. The goal with God is for us to have an absolutely pure (24-karat) faith!**

A Happy Ending

Chapter 42 of Job contains the epilogue (42:7-17). The first six verses quoted at the beginning of this chapter are Job's response to Yahweh at the end of His description of *Leviathan*. The epilogue has been interpreted variously as have been other critical parts of the book with the same diversity of opinions as we have discussed before. I take this chapter to be the necessary conclusion of Job's chronicle, which to many seems to be incredible. Robert Fyall observed this skepticism and remarked, "Few take seriously the immense importance of this chapter for a final assessment of the theology of the book."[75] Several reasons for the importance of this chapter present themselves after closer inspection. First, the reader needs to see the resolution of Job's relationship to *Yahweh*. Second, the sacrifice for and the forgiveness of Job's friends are needed to have closure to that aspect of the story. Third, every reader needs to understand the great love and grace involved for God to restore everything to Job double. Fourth, there is a real need to show the reconciliation of Job's immediate family and peripheral friends. In other words, the epilogue brings real closure to Job's story on several levels.

Job's final restoration on first observation may appear to confirm the doctrine of retribution in that

God seemingly rewarded Job for his faithful endurance. That interpretation ignores a major factor of Job's relation to God. The challenge of *the Satan* was that Job served God for reward, not "for nought" (1:9). **Job proved that he had not served God for blessing or reward.** Through all he suffered, Job had remained faithful to serve God and trust Him with his whole life even when no blessings were coming his way. **God was still under no obligation to reward Job, as retribution would require. Yet, in love and grace, God gave a double blessing.** Gregory Parsons stated this truth simply and to the point, "...in actuality this restoration was not a reward or payment but a free gift based solely on God's sovereign grace."[76] **Here, in the heart of the Old Testament, which is not given to such teachings, is one of the most beautiful expressions of the "grace" so clearly taught in Paul's writings:**

> Therefore, as ye abound in every thing, in faith, and utterance, and knowledge, and in all diligence, and in your love to us, see that ye abound in this grace also.
> -2 Corinthians 8:7

> Moreover the law entered, that the offence might abound. But where sin abounded, grace did much more abound:
> -Romans 5:20

> And God is able to make all grace abound toward you; that ye, always having all sufficiency in all

things, may abound to every good work:
-2 Corinthians 9:8

In these New Testament verses, **we see that our Father's provision is always based in His grace. He loves in grace; He provides in grace; He prospers in grace; He even allows a Job syndrome in grace.**

Job was unaware of the fact that he served God "for naught," at least, before and during the trial. From the beginning of his syndrome, he believed in the doctrine of retribution. He believed he was blessed because he had been faithful. He also believed that he was being unjustly punished because in self-examination he could not identify any sin, which should result in such calamity as he was experiencing. **By the biblical end of the story in chapter 42, Job's pat theology had been modified. He no longer thought of God as explainable or predictable. His spiritual eye now sees God as mysteriously holy, triumphantly sovereign and incalculably powerful in all His thoughts and designs, means and ways, as well as His purposes and ends.** This God of relationship, *Yahweh*, now was held in awe and worship in a way Job had not previously imagined. As Royce said earlier in his testimony, "…it was the worst thing that ever happened to me, but it was the best thing that ever happened to me…it was the best thing."

Meeting God always moves one from abstract ideas, explanations, descriptions, philosophical arguments and rationalizations, to the calm and confident acceptance of the Father Who is all-loving, all-caring and all-beneficent. **Relational motivation will trump intellectual or conceptual motivation eventually. Job had experienced his fill of human wisdom and rationale, even religious intellect.** He realized that he was a major contributor to this pool of the superfluous. **All he wanted or needed at this point was to bask, revel and regenerate in the Person of the whirlwind, his God and his Redeemer.**

Several other aspects of Job's restoration deserve comment. Job had mentioned that he was afraid of the terror of God (9:34; 13:21), but he still wanted to meet with God face to face and present his cause to Him. Norman Habel observed that the word "face" (*panim*) basically means presence, and it is a theme in several of Job's speeches (chapters 13 and 23).[77] It is amazing that God did not immediately respond to Job's demand, but He hid His "face" (3:24; cf. 23:9, 15, 17). Ultimately, God did appear to Job, and instead of responding to Job's challenge, He challenged Job. When *Yahweh* finished His revelation of Himself to Job, Job confessed having spoken out of presumption of knowledge, which was only ignorance. Habel explained it well while discussing "wisdom" in Job:

> Job has "found" the God he sought to "see" (23:9). Thus, Job may lack the wisdom which derives from a primordial knowledge of the principle governing Yahweh's design for the cosmos, but he gains first-hand knowledge through the theophany of the whirlwind. He did not find wisdom, but he found God...Job sees God and survives![78]

A cautionary word about Job's example and God's ways is necessary. **Not every case of the Job syndrome ends in a beautiful restoration and an easy death.** Abel, Uriah, Naboth, the martyred ones of Hebrews 11, and the martyred ones of the New Testament—all of these testify to tragic endings of life, which were not changed by God. Just recently, Mrs. Smith, a close acquaintance of mine, wasted away in a painful dying with cancer. She was a real saint. Explanations are beyond human understanding; they are in God's sovereign will. **The truth remains that the Joban principles of response will bring one to a good end, either here and now in life experience, or in His presence forever. Job's attitude cannot be improved. He declared adamantly, "Though he slay me, yet will I trust in him"** (Job 13:15a).

MY PRAYER

Great and loving Father of all who are Your adoring but needy children, I am awed at Your "higher than the earth" ways. My experience too often greatly exceeds my abilities. Yet, I know, according to Your Word, when I am weak, You really are strong. As I reduce myself emotionally and spiritually to sackcloth and ashes, teach me to trust You alone, just like You taught Job and Linda. I pause in the recording of these precious insights to love, to thank and to worship You for this privilege to share Who You are with others. To You, my Father, be all glory and honor both now and forever. Amen!

8
FATHER DOES KNOW BEST

> At this my heart pounds
> > and leaps from its place.
> Listen! Listen to the roar of his voice,
> > to the rumbling that comes from his mouth.
> He unleashes his lightning beneath the whole heaven
> > and sends it to the ends of the earth.
> After that comes the sound of his roar;
> > he thunders with his majestic voice.
> > When his voice resounds,
> > he holds nothing back.
> God's voice thunders in marvelous ways;
> > he does great things beyond our understanding.
> > > -Job 37:1-5 (NIV)

Throughout this writing, I have emphasized that God's sovereignty takes precedence over all else. Elihu, in his passionate speech to Job and his three friends partially quoted above, clearly held God and His sovereignty in the highest regard. He said that his heart was pounding as he contemplated God's majesty. He realized God's ways are marvelous (read "hidden"), and His works are so great as to be past our appreciation, seeing, perception, observation, recognition, and comprehension, in other words, our ability to know fully. Once again, **faith is necessary** to accept and receive our God Who is too marvelous for words.

As you go through a Job syndrome, the bedrock foundation of your faith is always Who God really is. You must, in every moment of the suffering, believe that He is, and that He is a rewarder (Hebrews 11:6). With Job, no matter what the circumstances look like or feel like, trust Him anyhow as you wait and wait and wait some more.

The Art of Waiting

James, the Apostle, after decades of leading the new first century Church, and suffering persecution, at the hands of the Jews and the Romans, clearly saw the need for the art of waiting, when under the inspiration of the Holy Spirit, he said this:

> Take, my brethren, the prophets, who have spoken in the name of the Lord, for an example of suffering affliction, and of patience. Behold, we count them happy which endure. Ye have heard of the patience of Job, and have seen the end of the Lord; that the Lord is very pitiful, and of tender mercy.
>
> -James 5:10-11

As it is used here, the word "patience" speaks of patient endurance through difficult and trying times, not some nebulous personality trait. At times, we are forced by circumstances to wait on the Lord. **While at other times,**

we need to choose to wait in quiet acceptance of what God is working.

We do not often consider that waiting may have real benefits. Almost any association one can make with the word "wait" will come up negative in nature: like, waiting on the wife to finish shopping; like, waiting on the husband to get that "honey-do" done; like, waiting on graduating from high school; like, waiting on someone to get out of the bathroom; like, waiting in the doctor's office. We generally think of waiting in this way. Our activity is being delayed while another's activity takes precedence. This delay on our part is most often seen as being negative, a "waste of time," unless we can utilize our delay time in a more creative way. It is so in the natural realm that we have developed many alternative ways to turn these negative "waitings" into something more beneficial to us. We can utilize those times for resting, planning, entertaining ourselves, or any of hundreds of other ways. Today with smart phones, tablets, and laptop computers we have run out of excuses for not using our wait time for something creative.

In the spiritual realm, however, waiting should take on a more positive meaning in our lives. In a world of instant everything, we would do well to learn something about the "patience of Job." The Bible has much to say about waiting. Carefully consider the following:

> If a man dies, shall he live again?
> All the days of my hard service I will wait,

Till my change comes.
-Job 14:14 (NKJV)

Wait on the Lord;
Be of good courage,
And He shall strengthen your heart;
Wait, I say, on the Lord!
-Psalm 27:14 (NKJV)

So you, by the help of your God, return;
Observe mercy and justice,
And wait on your God continually.
-Hosea 12:6 (NKJV)

But those who wait on the Lord
Shall renew their strength;
They shall mount up with wings like eagles,
They shall run and not be weary,
They shall walk and not faint.
-Isaiah 40:31 (NKJV)

For evildoers shall be cut off;
But those who wait on the Lord,
They shall inherit the earth."
-Psalm 37:9 (NKJV)

Not only that, but we also who have the firstfruits of the Spirit, even we ourselves groan within ourselves, eagerly waiting for the adoption, the redemption of our body.
-Romans 8:23 (NKJV)

…so that you come short in no gift, eagerly waiting

for the revelation of our Lord Jesus Christ...
-1 Corinthians 1:7 NKJV

But if we hope for what we do not see, we eagerly wait for it with perseverance.
-Romans 8:25 (NKJV)

We can see clearly from a biblical perspective that waiting should carry many benefits and blessings such as discipline, strength, courage, inheritance, healing, redemption and, ultimately, the coming of Christ. These are but a few of the positive results of a Christian life devoted to patiently waiting on God's will and empowerment.

I recently had another lesson in waiting. The following is the account as I wrote it that day:

> Here I sit on a hospital bed waiting for a cardiologist to tell me whether I need a procedure today for a malfunctioning pacemaker. I am just five weeks and six days from the surgical insertion of the pacer. Once again, I had enjoyed about four weeks of reprieve from the slow heartrate that had previously plagued me with weakness and, also, the suffering due to the soreness from surgery. Then seemingly out of nowhere came this trial of misery from 7:10 AM yesterday until now, 26 hours later. I have found that pacers are smart but fallible electronic devices. I have also discovered that a fluctuating heartrate from 45 to over 120 will make one feel lousy to a high degree. My rear end can testify that emergency room beds have way too little padding. Why is it that you just cannot get warm in

an ER? Why are there no lounge chairs for a caring wife to have a place to rest? And, here is this question for God, why does time stand still when one is suffering?

I have found out the electrical system of my heart is not in the healthiest condition. The pacer was basically misfiring due to over-sensing the parameters it deciphers. After a re-programming of the unit, I am feeling better for which I am truly grateful. Now, if I can just avoid the possibility of having to get a three-wire pacer!

I have determined I will follow Job's example and trust my Father completely. Yes, here I sit still waiting! I, too, am like Job—waiting! I find myself speaking about things too wonderful for me. Many of these things I still do not understand as God's ways are so much higher than my ways and thoughts.

I do know, here today, I have been impacted by a forceful new understanding of 1 Peter 2:20, "For what glory is it, if, when ye be buffeted for your faults, ye shall take it patiently? but if, when ye do well, and suffer for it, ye take it patiently, this is acceptable with God." Just for a moment, forget the glory and faults. **The buffeting for faults is a given, but when you have done "well" and yet "suffer for it," very serious questions are raised.** The phrase "this is acceptable" has overwhelmed me. What? **When we react patiently in undeserved suffering, God is pleased, and that reaction is acceptable to God!** I am learning today that I have not been very patient. Yes, I was patient when the nurse did not bring me water for several hours. I was even patient when an EMT tried again and again to get an IV started but failed. I showed a degree of grace several times through this ordeal, but inside I was not very patient with my loving heavenly Father. When from this fantastic verse in Peter's letter I realized I was missing the approval of the Lord of glory, I became even more miserable with my failure to suffer patiently.

Organized Attacks

There is an "organized attack" that occurs (A concept from international evangelist, Sherlock Bally).[79] It seems to come from all directions at once. **The nature of the conflict is supernatural and therefore the resolution of it is supernatural.** As in Job's case, his God-experience came in the attack and that was a supernatural resolution to his problems. His life became doubly blessed. **When the enemy of our souls accuses, we can know that God thinks very highly of us and trusts us if He allows** *the Satan* **to attack.**

The first wave of attack on Job did not move him from his position of faith in God. So, immediately *the Satan* sought permission for a physical attack. Job experienced the four-pronged attack of loss of wealth, loss of children, discouragement of his wife and the loss of his health. This illustrates what is meant by "organized attack." **The source of the attack was supernatural but the effect of it was natural.** In other words, Job felt the effects in the natural realm. **Since the source was supernatural, the deliverance and healing would also be supernatural.** We need to remind ourselves that from Job's perspective the confrontation going on in the spirit world was being experienced in a very real and painful way in Job's natural world. He did not see nor could he know at any level about *the Satan's* challenge to God. Neither did he receive any comfort from the fact, which was unknown to him, that God had expressed such great confidence in his faithfulness.

In reading the book of Job, it is easy to see that **God had everything under control**, but Job did not know that in an experiential way. He only knew by faith that God was supposed to be that kind of God. It is the same way when we go through a Job syndrome. **We can only perceive our painful experience, but that is the place and time that faith must reach out in confidence to El Shaddai, the Almighty.**

Hear Job cry out, "Though he slay me, yet will I trust in him…" (Job 13:15) What confidence in God! What faith! Not knowing that God had already limited the attack of *the Satan*, yet **Job knew what he knew—God has ultimate control!** Hear the rest of Job's statement:

> Though he slay me, yet will I trust in him: but I will maintain mine own ways before him. He also shall be my salvation: for an hypocrite shall not come before him. Hear diligently my speech, and my declaration with your ears. Behold now, I have ordered my cause; I know that I shall be justified.
> -Job 13:15-18

This is the kind of faith that will be necessary to go through a Job syndrome. We need to repeat after Job:

1. I will trust Him.
2. I will walk in righteousness before Him.
3. He is and will be my salvation.
4. Hypocrites have no audience with God.
5. I have maintained my cause.
6. I shall be justified.

When, like Job's faith, my faith is set like a flint in confidence of Who God is and a determination of who I am before Him, the Job syndrome, no matter how difficult, will not shake this faith or cause it to waver. The Satan's "organized attack" may cause damage, loss, pain and heartache, but it cannot destroy or even bend this kind of faith. At this level of faith, one is very near 24-karat faith!

> But he knoweth the way that I take: when he hath tried me, I shall come forth as gold.
> —Job 23:10

Insight from Outside Christian Writing

In 1945 Robert Frost, one of the most celebrated American poets, wrote a short play entitled "A Masque of Reason." It is in the form of a poem in blank verse. The play is a dialogue between Job, God, Job's wife, and eventually *the Satan* joins the ensemble. The setting is a thousand years later. The ending line is, "Here endeth Chapter Forty-three of Job."[80] Since there are only forty-two chapters in Job, Frost is projecting a tongue-in-cheek humorous exchange between the characters, which might be an explanation as to the reason for the book of Job. Frost wrote an insightful speech by God in response to Job as He described Job's past experience. Frost's concept was that **Job's ordeal had to make no sense in order ultimately to make sense.** He believed that Job's suffering really changed theological thought by reinterpreting the law of retribution as set forth in Deuteronomy. In the speech, God even thanks Job for liberating Him from a "mortal bondage" to humankind, then God revealed a fascinating concept. In retribution as traditionally taught, God's free will is limited, because man's is unlimited. According to Frost, God was saying to Job that it was man…

> Who could do good or evil as he chose.
> I had no choice but I must follow him
> With forfeits and rewards he understood –
> Unless I liked to suffer loss of worship.
> I had to prosper good and punish evil.
> You changed all that. You set me free to reign.
> You are the emancipator of your God –
> And as such I promote you to a saint.[81]

Frost clearly recognized the conflict in Job of the Deuteronomist's doctrine of retribution and the reality of Job suffering innocently. I think it is time that all of those going through a Job syndrome and their "friends" learn to be emancipators of God. The truth is **God will never live in our box of expectations! He does not submit to our**

molding Him in our image. He remains the Potter. We must move to where He is through faith.

Deep Things Out of Darkness (Job 12:22)

From the beginning of this writing the goal has been to focus on Job's experience of suffering, his wrestling with God's seeming abandonment of justice, and a confrontation by Yahweh Himself. Job's "complex of symptoms," which indicated his "undesirable condition" (see chapter 1) were, in fact, the syndrome, which attaches itself to some of God's most extraordinarily proficient children. Why God is willing, seemingly, to risk the failure of His children in order to see them conquer and win is a mystery, which will remain. **He has a greater purpose, but we all will continue to try to "divine" the "Mystery of Misery." Every time one of God's own sons or daughters participates with Him in fighting *the Satan* and the evil he initiates and propagates, God is blessed, and His Kingdom moves forward.** The Apostle Paul put it this way in his letter to the church at Thessalonica:

> Therefore, among God's churches we boast about your perseverance and faith in all the persecutions and trials you are enduring. All this is evidence that God's judgment is right, and as a result you will be counted worthy of the kingdom of God, for which you are suffering. God is just: He will pay back trouble to those who trouble you and give relief to you who are troubled, and to us as well. This will

happen when the Lord Jesus is revealed from heaven in blazing fire with his powerful angels.
                                   -2 Thessalonians 1:4-7 (NIV)

Paul declared here that there will be a setting right of all the wrongs. Evil against us will be dealt with by the Lord Jesus Himself. The Job syndrome will lose its grasp eternally. We will be free!

Job has proven by his life and faith that it is possible for a man to serve God and worship Him without ulterior motive. With Job, believers, in their own crucible, may discover the freedom and ecstasy of having learned to serve *Yahweh* **"for nought" (1:9).** Those in the Job syndrome may learn to worship purely even when facing the most miserable of conditions. Every believer experiencing the bitter affliction of the Job syndrome, like Job, can move from walking among the "deep things out of darkness" (12:22) to the brilliance and glory of the most fantastic revelation of *Yahweh* exclaiming "now my eye sees You!" (42:5, NASB)

A Final Word

Job confessed one wrong. He talked too much. He said that he had talked about things of which he really had no knowledge. Now that is something that we all could confess. It seems every one of us has this interminable characteristic of not wanting to seem ignorant, so we bluff our way through some conversations with our more-or-less partial knowledge. **Job did not see himself as a bloviator**

until he stood in the Presence within the whirlwind. In the revealing brightness of God's moral perfection, Job saw clearly his own need to be quiet. The Apostle Peter made this relevant comment on how we are to be adorned:

> But let it be the hidden man of the heart, in that which is not corruptible, even the ornament of a meek and quiet spirit, which is in the sight of God of great price.
> -1 Peter 3:4

No matter how righteously one has lived, in the Presence, every humanesque (fleshly) part of us seems so unworthy of being there. **That which is humanly "good" is bound to fall far short of His holy, holy, holy goodness. Numerous saints of the Scripture had this Job-like experience of encountering God. In every case, that encounter changed the person forever.** Moses, Jacob, Isaiah and Saul of Tarsus are just a few who were permanently disabled in their own ability yet enabled in God's power and authority to impact their generation in profound ways. Their resulting contributions to God's revelation of His way and will for mankind still impact us today as they have through the generations of three millenniums.

In becoming aware of himself in the light of God's glory, Job humbled himself, "I abhor myself, and repent in dust and ashes." (Job 42:6) Think of that! The man, who had already been humbled by losses of wealth, children, position and health to the point of having nothing and being a nobody, still humbled himself in dust and ashes—**worshipping**!!! Perhaps that is the weightiest lesson for us to learn in our response to God.

Even now, I shut my mouth, or in this case, quit typing the keys of this computer…to sit dumb…in the **Presence**…

MY PRAYER

Oh! Holy Father, once again I am at the end of myself. You are profoundly present. I find myself as a worm. Please forgive my presumption to write of You and Your servant Job. Yet, use these frail human words, which I am confident You have motivated, to touch the hearts of the readers. May You, Father, bring each of us into a similar Job-like encounter with You… I yield! I desire Your Presence more than I want what I want. I humbly wait for You to move through me with the next revelation of the Truth…Amen!

NOTES

[1] David J. A. Clines, *Job 1-20*, Word Biblical Commentary, vol. 17 (Nashville: Nelson Reference Electronic, 1989), 215.

[2] *American Heritage Dictionary of the English Language*, 4th ed., s.v. "Syndrome."

[3] Claude E. Cox, "When Torah Embraced Wisdom and Song: Job 28:8, Ecclesiastes 12:13 and Psalm 1:2" *Restoration Quarterly* 49, no. 2 (2007): 65-74, online database available from http://firstsearch.oclc.org (accessed March 12, 2009).

[4] Robert L. Alden, *Job,* The New American Commentary series, vol. 11, CD-ROM, Logos Library System (electronic ed., 2001), under "Purpose" (Nashville, TN: Broadman & Holman Publishers, 1993).

[5] Frances I. Anderson, *Job: An Introduction and Commentary*, The Tyndale Old Testament Commentaries, ed. D. J. Wiseman (Downers Grove, IL: Inter-Varsity Press, 1976), 65.

[6] From an interview with Ron and Vicki Trenum on March 6, 2014.

[7] Robert Gordis, *The Book of God and Man* (Chicago: University of Chicago Press, 1830), 7.

[8] James E. Smith, *The Wisdom Literature and Psalms*, Old Testament Survey Series, CD ROM, Libronix Digital Library System, under "Chapter Two, A Human Speculation" (Joplin, MO: College Press Pub. Co., 1995).

[9] Édouard Dhorme, *A Commentary of the Book of Job* (Nashville: Thomas Nelson, 1984), 1.

[10] Anderson, *Job: An Introduction and Commentary*, 78.

[11] Dhorme, *A Commentary of the Book of Job*, 1.

[12] Dhorme, *A Commentary of the Book of Job*, 1.

[13] Dhorme, *A Commentary of the Book of Job*, 2.

[14] Dhorme, *A Commentary of the Book of Job*, 2.

[15] Dhorme, *A Commentary of the Book of Job*, xxxviii.

[16] Dhorme, *A Commentary of the Book of Job*, 19.

[17] Anderson, *Job: An Introduction and Commentary*, 96.

[18] Dhorme, *A Commentary of the Book of Job*, 649.

[19] Alden, *Job*, under "Literary Style."

[20] Dhorme, *A Commentary of the Book of Job*, xx-xxi.

[21] The reader might compare the changes in English from Shakespeare until now, a period of four hundred years, while having book-making to proliferate, which helps preserve the language forms.

[22] Gordis, *The Book of God and Man*, 43.

[23] This address was given at the memorial of Troy L. Miller, D.D. August 10, 2011 by John R. Miller, D.Min.

[24] Marvin H. Pope, *Job*, The Anchor Bible, vol. 15 (New York: Doubleday & Company, 1965), xxiv.

[25] G. W. Leibniz, *Theodicy: Essays on the Goodness of God, the Freedom of Man, and the Origin of Evil*, trans. E. M. Huggard (La Salle, IL: Open Court, 1985).

[26] Walter Brueggemann, "Some Aspects of Theodicy in Old Testament Faith," *Perspectives in Religious Studies* 26, no. 3 (Fall 1999): 266.

[27] Vij Sodera, MD, interview by author via telephone and e-mail, May 22, 2009.

[28] J. F. Walvoord, R. Zuck and Dallas Theological Seminary, *The Bible Knowledge Commentary: An exposition of the Scriptures*, CD-ROM, Libronix Digital Library System, under "Job" (Wheaton, IL: Victor Books, 1985).

NOTES

[29] Walvoord and Zuck, *The Bible Knowledge Commentary,* "Job."

[30] Smith, *The Wisdom Literature*, under "Chapter Two, A Human Speculation."

[31] Robert Gordis, *The Book of Job: Commentary, New Translation, Special Studies* (New York: The Jewish Theological Seminary Press, 2012), 98.

[32] From a recorded interview with Dale Croft, June 4, 2016.

[33] J. Gabriel Miller, "Ultimate Reality" (unpublished, 2016), 18.

[34] Dhorme, *A Commentary of the Book of Job*, cliv-clxviii.

[35] John E. Hartley, *The Book of Job*, The New International Commentary of the Old Testament (Grand Rapids, MI: William B. Eerdmans Publishing Company, 1988), 171.

[36] David Wolfers, *Deep Things Out of Darkness: The Book of Job: Essays and a New English Translation.* (Grand Rapids: William B. Eerdmans Publishing, 1995), 77.

[37] Hartley, *The Book of Job*, 210-11.

[38] Robert S. Fyall, *Now my Eyes Have Seen You: Images of Creation and Evil in the Book of Job* (Downers Grove, IL: Intervarsity Press, 2002), 177.

[39] Hartley, *The Book of Job*, 534.

[40] Pope, *Job,* The Anchor Bible, lxxvii.

[41] Pope, *Job,* The Anchor Bible, lxxvii.

[42] Pope, *Job,* The Anchor Bible, lxxii-lxxviii.

[43] Hartley, *Book of Job*, 315.

[44] Hartley, *Book of Job*, 316.

[45] Hartley, *Book of Job*, 316.

[46] Dhorme, *A Commentary of the Book of Job*, cxxviii. Dhorme's statement is certainly debatable when compared to God's love, mercy, and grace.

[47] Anderson, *Job: An Introduction and Commentary*, 64.

[48] Anderson, *Job: An Introduction and Commentary*, 64.

[49] Anderson, *Job: An Introduction and Commentary*, 68.

[50] Anderson, *Job: An Introduction and Commentary*, 69.

[51] Hartley, *The Book of Job*, 71.

[52] Hartley, *The Book of Job*, 71.

[53] Dwight A. Pryor, e-mail message to author, March 25, 2009. Quote from C. S. Lewis, *The Lion, the Witch and the Wardrobe: A Story for Children* (New York, NY: MacMillan Publishing Company, 1950), 149.

[54] Recorded interview with Royce and Marie Dias, December 13, 2014.

[55] Hartley, *The Book of Job*, 173.

[56] Wolfers, *Deep Things,* 165-67.

[57] Wolfers, *Deep Things,* 166.

[58] Norman C. Habel, *The Book of Job*, The Old Testament Library series (Philadelphia: The Westminster Press, 1985), 558.

[59] Fyall, *Now My Eyes*, 139.

[60] Hartley, *The Book of Job*, 71.

[61] Hartley, *The Book of Job*, 530.

[62] Gordis, *The Book of God and Man*, 156.

[63] David B. Burrell, *Deconstructing Theodicy: Why Job Has Nothing to Say to the Puzzle of Suffering* (Grand Rapids: Brazos Press, 2008), 132.

[64] Gordis, *The Book of God and Man*, 156.

[65] Recorded interview with Sarah Tucker, June 10, 2014.

[66] Recorded interview with Linda Blore, November 21, 2014.

[67] William C. Williams, *Evangelical Dictionary of Biblical Theology*, CD-ROM, Biblesoft, Inc., under "Evil" (Grand Rapids, MI: Baker Books, 1996).

NOTES

[68] William C. Williams, *Evangelical Dictionary,* under "Evil".

[69] Friedrich Buchsel, "thumos, epithumia, etc. (transliterated by writer)," *Theological Dictionary of the New Testament*, vol. III, ed. Gerhard Kittel, trans. Geoffrey W. Bromiley (Grand Rapids, MI: Wm. B. Eerdmans Publishing Company, 1965), 165-72.

[70] Wolfers, *Deep Things,* 318.

[71] André Lacocque, "The Deconstruction of Job's Fundamentalism," *Journal of Biblical Literature* 126 (Spring 2007): 83-97.

[72] Gordis, *The Book of God and Man*, 86.

[73] Gordis, *The Book of God and Man*, 87.

[74] Hartley, *The Book of Job*, 339.

[75] Fyall, *Now My Eyes*, 175.

[76] Gregory W. Parsons, "The Structure and Purpose of the Book of Job," *Biliotheca Sacra* 138 (April-June 1981): 139-57.

[77] Norman C. Habel, "Of Things Beyond Me: Wisdom in the Book of Job," *Currents In Theology and Mission* 10, no. 3 (June 1983): 154.

[78] Habel, "Of Things Beyond Me," 154.

[79] From a private conversation with Sherlock Bally, January 29, 2018.

[80] Robert Frost, "A Masque of Reason," *The Poetry of Robert Frost*, ed. Edward Connery Lathem (New York, NY: Chicago, IL: San Francisco, CA: Holt, Rinehart and Winston, 1969), 490.

[81] Frost, "A Masque of Reason," 475-76.

SELECTED BIBLIOGRAPHY

Alden, Robert L. *Job*. The New American Commentary. Vol. 11. CD-ROM, 2001. Libronix Digital Library System. Nashville, TN: Broadman Press, 1993.

Anderson, Francis I. *Job: An Introduction and Commentary*. The Tyndale Old Testament Commentaries. Edited by D. Wiseman. Downers Grove, IL: Inter-Varsity Press, 1976.

Archer, G. L. *A Survey of Old Testament Introduction*. 3rd ed. CD-ROM. Libronix Digital Library System. Under "Date of Events." Chicago, IL: Moody Press, 1994.

Balentine, Samuel E. *Job*. Smyth & Helwys Bible Commentary. Macon, GA: Smyth & Helwys Publishing, 2006.

———. "For no reason." *Interpretation* 57, no. 4 (October 2003): 349-69. http://firstsearch.oclc.org (accessed June 8, 2009).

———. "Who Will Be Job's Redeemer." *Perspectives in Religious Studies* 26, no. 3 (Fall 1999): 269-89. http://firstsearch.oclc.org (accessed June 12, 2009).

Boadt, Lawrence, ed. *The Book of Job: Why Do the Innocent Suffer?* New York, NY: St. Marti's Griffin, 1999.

Brueggemann, Walter. "Some Aspects of Theodicy in Old Testament Faith." *Perspectives in Religious Studies* 26, no. 3 (Fall 1999): 253-68. http://firstsearch.oclc.org (accessed June 12, 2009).

———. "Theodicy in a social dimension." *Journal for the Study of the Old Testament* 33 (October 1985): 3-25. http://firstsearch.oclc.org (accessed June 8, 2009).

Buchsel, Friedrich. *Theological Dictionary of the New Testament*, Vol. 3. Edited by Gerhard Kittel. Translated by Geoffrey W. Bromily. Grand Rapids, MI: Wm. B. Eerdmans Publishing Company, 1965.

Burrell, David B. *Deconstructing Theodicy: Why Job Has Nothing to Say to the Puzzle of Suffering*. Grand Rapids, MI: Brazos Press, 2008.

Carson, D. A. *New Bible Commentary*: 21st edition. 4th ed. CD-ROM, 2001. Libronix Digital Library System. Downers Grove, IL: Inter-Varsity Press, 1994.

Clines, David J. A. *Job 1-20*. Word Biblical Commentary. Vol. 17. Nashville, TN: Nelson Reference Electronic, 1989.

———. *Job 21-37*. Word Biblical Commentary. Vol. 18. Nashville, TN: Thomas Nelson Publishers, 2006.

———. "Does the Book of Job Suggest that Suffering is Not a Problem?" Article online. Available at http://www.shef.ac.uk/bibs/DJACcurries/ProblemSuffering.pdf (accessed April 17, 2009).

Cooper, Burton Z. "Why, God: a Tale of Two Sufferers." *Theology Today* 42, no. 4 (January 1986): 423-34. http://firstsearch.oclc.org (accessed June 8, 2009).

Cox, Claud E. "When Torah embraced wisdom and song: Job 28:8, Ecclesiastes 12:13, and Psalm 1:2." *Restoration Quarterly* 49, no. 2 (2007): 65-74. http://firstsearch.oclc.org (accessed March 12, 2009).

Dhorme, Edouard. *A Commentary of the Book of Job*. Translated by Harold Knight. Nashville, TN: Thomas Nelson Publishers, 1967.

Driver, S. R., and G. B. Gray. *A Critical and Exegetical Commentary on the Book of Job together with a New Translation*. Edinburgh: T. & T. Clark, 1921.

Edwards. D. Miall. "Affliction." In *International Standard Bible Encyclopaedia*. Edited by James Orr. Biblesoft, Inc. Electronic Database, 2003. Chicago, IL: The Howard-Severance Company, 1915.

SELECTED BIBLIOGRAPHY

Epstein, Rabbi Dr. I., ed. Contents of the Soncino Babylonian Talmud. London: The Soncino Press, N.d. Under "Baba Bathra 14b." http://www.come-andhear.om/bababathra/bababathra_14.html (accessed May 4, 2009).

Frost, Robert. "A Masque of Reason." In *The Poetry of Robert Frost.* Edited by Edward Connery Lathem. New York, NY: Chicago, IL: San Francisco, CA: Holt, Rinehart and Winston, 1969.

Fyall, Robert S. *Now My Eyes Have Seen You: Images of Creation and Evil in the Book of Job.* Downers Grove, IL: Intervarsity Press, 2002.

Geisler, N. L., and W. E. Nix. *A General Introduction to the Bible.* Revised and expanded. CD-ROM. Libronix Digital Library System. Under "The Medieval Church." Chicago, IL: Moody Press, 1996.

Gibson, John C. L. *Job.* The Daily Study Bible Series. CD-ROM. Libronix Digital Library System. Under "Introduction." Louisville, KY: Westminster John Knox Press, 1985.

Gordis, Robert. *The Book of God and Man: A Study of Job.* Chicago, IL: University of Chicago Press, 1965.

———. *The Book of Job: Commentary, New Translation, and Special Studies.* New York, NY: The Jewish Theological Seminary of America, 1978.

Gorringe, Timothy. "Job and the Pharisees." *Interpretation* 40, no. 1 (January 1986): 17-28. http://firstsearch.oclc.org (accessed June 8, 2009).

Habel, Norman C. "Of Things Beyond Me: Wisdom in the Book of Job." *Currents in Theology and Mission* 10, no. 3 (June 1983): 142-54. http://firstsearch.oclc.org (accessed March 12, 2009).

———. *The Book of Job.* The Old Testament Library. Edited by Peter Ackroyd et al. Philadelphia: The Westminster Press, 1985.

Hartley, John E. *The Book of Job.* The New International Commentary on the Old Testament. Grand Rapids, MI: William B. Eerdmans Publishing Company, 1988.

Holmes, A. F. "Aquinas, Thomas (1225-1274)." In *Who's Who in Christian History*. Edited by J. D. Douglas, P. W. Comfort, and D. Mitchell. CD-ROM. Libronix Digital Library System. Wheaton, IL: Tyndale House, 1997.

Keil, C. F., and F. Delitzsch. *Commentary on the Old Testament*. CD-ROM. Libronix Digital Library System. Peabody, MA: Hendrickson, 2002.

Klein, Ralph W. "No Easy Answers." *Currents in Theology and Mission* 34 (October 2007): 325-37. http://firstsearch.oclc.org (accessed March 12, 2009).

Lacocque, André. "The Deconstruction of Job's Fundamentalism." *Journal of Biblical Literature* 126 (Spring 2007): 83-97. http://firstsearch.oclc.org (accessed March 12, 2009).

———. "Job or the Impotence of Religion and Philosophy." *Semeia* 19 (1981): 33-52. Edited by J. D. Crossan. Chicago, IL: Scholars Press. http://firstsearch.oclc.org (accessed March 12, 2009).

Leibniz, G. W. *Theodicy: Essays on the Goodness of God, the Freedom of Man, and the Origin of Evil*. La Salle, IL: Open Court, 1985.

Lewis, C. S. *The Lion, the Witch and the Wardrobe: A Story for Children*. New York, NY: MacMillan Publishing Company, 1950.

Long, Thomas G. "Job: Second Thoughts in the Land of Uz." *Theology Today* 45, no.1(April 1988): 5-20. http://firstsearch.oclc.org (accessed June 8, 2009).

Nuyen, A. T. "The 'Ethical Anthropic Principle' and the Religious Ethics of Levinas." *Journal of Religious Ethics* 29, no. 3 (Fall 2001): 427-42. http://firstsearch.oclc.org (accessed June 12, 2009).

O'Brien, Dennis. "Prolegomena to a dissolution to the problem of Suffering." *Harvard Theological Review* 57, no. 4 (October 1964): 301-23. http://firstsearch. oclc.org (accessed June 8, 2009).

O'Brien, J. Randall. "World, Winds, and Whirlwinds: the Voice of God Meets 'The Vice of God.'" *Perspectives in Religious Studies* 30, no. 2 (Summer 2003): 151-60. http://firstsearch.oclc.org (accessed June 8, 2009).

SELECTED BIBLIOGRAPHY

Orlinsky, Harry Meyer. "Studies in the Septuagint of the Book of Job." *Hebrew Union College Annual* 32 (1961): 239-68. http://firstsearch.oclc.org (accessed March 12, 2009).

Parsons, Gregory W. "The Structure and Purpose of the Book of Job." *Biliotheca Sacra* 138 (April-June 1981): 139-57. http://firstsearch.oclc.org (accessed May 15, 2009).

Pippin, Tina. "Job 42:1-6, 10-17." *Interpretation* 53, no. 3 (July 1999): 299-303. http://firstsearch.oclc.org (accessed June 8, 2009).

Pope, Marvin H. *Job.* The Anchor Bible. Vol. 15. Garden City, NY: Doubleday and Company, 1988.

Scheindlin, Raymond P. *The Book of Job: Translation, Introduction, and Notes.* New York, NY: W. W. Norton and Company, 1998.

Smith, James E. *The Wisdom Literature and Psalms.* Old Testament Survey Series. CD-ROM. Libronix Digital Library System. Under "Chapter Two, A Human Speculation." Joplin, MO: College Press Pub. Co., 1996.

Snaith, Norman H. *The Book of Job: Its Origin and Purpose.* Studies in Biblical Theology, Vol. 11. 1968; 2nd ed., London: SCM Press Ltd., 1972.

Tanakh: The Holy Scriptures. Jerusalem: The Jewish Publication Society, 1985.

Tsevat, Matitiahu. "The meaning of the book of Job." *Hebrew Union College Annual* 37 (1966): 73-106. http://firstsearch.oclc.org (accessed June 8, 2009).

Tur-Sinai, N. H. *The Book of Job: A New Commentary.* Jerusalem: Kiryat Sefer Ltd., 1967.

Vos, A. "Maimonides (Moses Ben Maimon) (1135-1204)." In *Who's Who in Christian History.* Edited by J. D. Douglas, P. W. Comfort, and D. Mitchell. CD-ROM. Libronix Digital Library System. Wheaton, IL: Tyndale House, 1997.

Walvoord, J. F., R. B. Zuck, and Dallas Theological Seminary. "Job." In *The Bible Knowledge Commentary: An Exposition of the Scriptures.*

CD-ROM. Libronix Digital Library System. Wheaton, IL: Victor Books, 1985.

Williams, Michael S. "The Book of Job as a Reflection on the Practice of Ministry." *Journal of Religious Thought* 54-55, no. 2 (Spring-Fall 1998): 53-9. http://firstsearch.oclc.org (accessed May 15, 2009).

Williams, William C. "Evil." In *Evangelical Dictionary of Biblical Theology*. CD-ROM. Biblesoft, Inc. Grand Rapids, MI: Baker Books, 1996.

Wolfers, David. *Deep Things Out of Darkness: The Book of Job: Essays and a New English Translation*. Grand Rapids, MI: William B. Eerdmans Publishing Company, 1995.

Young, Josiah U. "'Wonder What God Had in Mind?': Leibniz's Theodicy and the Art of Toni Morrison." *Black Theology* 5, no. 1 (2007): 63-80. http://firstsearch. oclc.org (accessed June 8, 2009).

ACKNOWLEDGEMENTS

The Job Syndrome has a precursor, a dissertation written for a doctoral degree. The acknowledgements in the original dissertation seem appropriate here to honor the people in my life who made this book possible. People really do need people, and I am no exception. A project of the nature of this writing requires so much time and effort that it would be nearly impossible to accomplish it alone. I want to express my sincere appreciation to those who have contributed time, effort, and encouragement.

The person who wins my Most Valuable vote is Paula, my faithful rib, who has had to learn quickly new software, formatting, and the precise detail necessary for the writing of a dissertation. Her encouragement, on the days when throwing in the towel seemed the only option for sanity, was then, and is now, a strong motivation. When writing this present book, her gifts of patience, help, and love were priceless.

Having recently earned his Ph.D. in music theory, my son, Gabriel, understood the process and gave great advice, as well as just being there when I needed to talk. His gifts of loving support and expertise were irreplaceable.

My brother, Troy, was a major motivator and facilitator from the beginning of the doctoral program, and continued as an inspiration until his untimely passing. Mom is not with us now, but she was there during the first part of the program. I know she is pleased with "our" accomplishment. My brother, Lemuel, and "Sis," Alethea, have also contributed their love and encouragements. Their gifts of faithfulness and caring were very precious.

At the beginning, the time element for completing the research and first phase of writing was pressing in until Pastor Timothy Miller released me from duties as an associate pastor to utilize a sabbatical to give my full time to the project. The gift of time was invaluable.

Two people, who deserve a special word of appreciation for the giving of their valuable time to be my research assistants, are Linda Anderson and Lynn VanBuren. Because of their tireless efforts, I was able to spend more time in thinking of how to convey Job's message. Their gift of selfless toil was of great worth.

The excellent faculty and staff of Beacon University went beyond their designated duties to be not only my erudite mentors, but also, my friends. Without the personal concern and direction of my professors and administrators, this book would not have come about. Their gifts of knowledge, time, and *agape* were and are inestimable.

The emotional and spiritual presence of all those faithful brothers and sisters, who have supported me with prayer and means, has been a great uplifting to the hands, which were wont to fall. I pray God's grace on each one of those dear ones in the congregations where I have served. Their gifts of support and fellowship are treasured.

Two others, whose contributions might seem small, but in fact, they have seasoned critical parts of the argument of this writing, are my friends and major stimulators of thought: Vij Sodera, M.D., an author from the United Kingdom, and Dr. Dwight Pryor, Hebrew scholar extraordinaire. Their gifts of reverent scholarship are rare.

A devout follower of Christ, a member of our congregation, an English scholar and a linguist of considerable expertise has given herself to the task of being my editor for this project. She is my friend, and just happens to be a cousin on my mother's side, Shelly Williams. Her gift of literary skill was so necessary.

In the process of writing this book, I experienced other Job syndromes, having been in the hospital several times and facing many hindrances to the work. But God! My God brought healing and peace (after I had some Job-like ranting) at just the right timing. His grace is beyond all human comprehension. To my heavenly Father, I give all honor and thanksgiving. His gifts are incredible.

To all those mentioned above, I give my deepest thanks and love!

www.ingramcontent.com/pod-product-compliance
Lightning Source LLC
Chambersburg PA
CBHW051822090426
42736CB00011B/1598